TEN THINGS I HATE ABOUT ME

TEN THINGS I HATE ABOUT ME

How to stay alive with a brain that's trying to kill you

Joe Tracini

TRAPEZE

First published in Great Britain in 2022 by Trapeze,
this paperback edition published in 2023 by Trapeze,
an imprint of The Orion Publishing Group Ltd
Carmelite House, 50 Victoria Embankment
London EC4Y 0DZ

An Hachette UK Company

3 5 7 9 10 8 6 4

A CIP catalogue record for this book is
available from the British Library.

ISBN (Mass Market Paperback) 978 1 3987 0594 4
ISBN (eBook) 978 1 3987 0595 1
ISBN (Audio) 978 1 3987 0596 8

Typeset by Input Data Services Ltd, Somerset

Printed and bound in Great Britain by Clays Ltd, Elcograf S.p.A.

www.orionbooks.co.uk

For Andy xx

'The unexamined life isn't worth living'
—Socrates

'Nobody cares about your shit life. You're going to die alone'
—the voice in my head

Contents

A Note from the Author   xi
The Rope Trick   xiii
Ten Things You Should Know about Mick   xxi
A Brief Interlude on Suicide   xxv

1. Unclear Sense of Self   1
2. Impulsive and Self-destructive Behaviour   31
3. Fear of Abandonment   67
4. Feelings of Suicide and Self-harm   89
5. Extreme Emotional Swings   109
6. Unstable Relationships   133
7. Explosive Anger   163
8. Chronic Feelings of Emptiness   177
9. Paranoia and Dissociation   191
10. Me   219

Ten Things I Love about You   235
Appendix   237
Acknowledgements   239
Credits   243

A Note from the Author

Hi. I hope you're OK.

I mean, you're probably not if you're reading this, but still, hi.

Before we get started, I need to warn you that this book is going to talk about suicide, including detailing suicidal methods. It's going to detail experience of sexual assault. It's also going to talk about addiction, including references to cocaine and alcohol abuse. It's going to examine self-harm and depression. It's going to be honest about some of the darkest things it's possible to feel. It's also going to (try to) be funny. I know some people will not be in a place where this is the right book for them to read. Please do what you need to do to be as safe as possible.

Some people may object to this mix of subject and approach on principle. I want to be clear that it's not my intention to make light of any of these things; as you'll see if you read the book, I'm well aware of their heaviness. I genuinely believe that the best way to open up a space to talk about what's going on in our heads is to speak frankly, using the full range of expression we use when discussing everything else. To have an important conversation without humour is like trying to paint a picture with only half the colours. You *can* do it but your picture is going to be shit.

Also, there's a reason the standard advice is to begin a speech with a joke. Because the person laughing and the person telling the joke become briefly part of the same shared universe. And once you've got them, they'll listen to you in a different way. I want the best chance of bringing you all into my universe. That means giving myself, at the very least, the same verbal equipment as every drunk best man ever.

So to conclude: I'm going to talk about suicide; please don't read this book if you're not in the right headspace for that, and I think we can all agree that the bride's mum looks absolutely stunning.

The Rope Trick

The trouble with being a suicidal magician is that it's remarkably hard to kill yourself.

It's 2013 and I am 24 years old, sat alone on the floor of my flat, surrounded by rope, but the only knot I know how to tie is one that would immediately come undone.

As this didn't feel like the sort of thing it felt appropriate to ask a friend or neighbour for help with, I googled '*How to tie a noose*' and found a suitable 90-second video. Everything I needed to know, set out step by step, and I was ready to follow the instructions. The only thing was that they'd put the Benny Hill music over it. As everyone knows, it's impossible not to laugh at the Benny Hill music and, in that moment, as I was laughing, something shifted and I stopped wanting to die.

There are two things I want to tell you – the first is that, contrary to portrayals on television, saving someone's life doesn't have to be a big dramatic leap, dragging them back from the edge of the bridge, or pulling them out of oncoming traffic. It can be an everyday thing, a small kindness whose impact stretches far beyond your understanding. Whoever made that video, you should know that your choice of soundtrack saved my life.

Borderline Personality Disorder

I live with Borderline Personality Disorder (BPD), a complex mental illness that affects nearly 1 per cent of the population. Your initial reaction is probably: 'One per cent? That's quite niche, you mental health hipster.' But that's a minimum of 670,000 people in the UK alone. A population bigger than the city of Glasgow. Every time you get on a crowded train, there are probably four or five of us on there with you.

When you have BPD, you have one job to do, *every single day*. Don't – whatever you do – die.

15 per cent of people with BPD die by suicide, and 40 per cent try. I'm already in the 40 per cent. My job is to keep out of the 15 per cent. It's so common for people with BPD to take their own lives that it's the only mental health problem that lists suicide as a symptom.

But that's not the only way it fucks with you.

You know how, on DVDs, you sometimes get the director's commentary? My brain with BPD is like that, except the director hates the film. HATES it. It's as though it's the worst thing they've ever done, and they're being forced to watch it over and over and over and over again for ever. I live with my BPD providing a running commentary of my life, and hating every second of it. But not only that – every moment this commentary is trying to convince me to turn the volume up too high, too low, make the contrast weird, turn on Russian subtitles, throw the remote control through the window and, eventually, eject the DVD way before the film is over.

The nine symptoms of BPD as described in The American Psychiatric Association's *The Diagnostic and Statistical Manual of Mental Disorders, Fifth Edition* are: an unclear or shifting sense of self; impulsive and self-destructive behaviour; fear of abandonment; feelings of suicide and self-harm; extreme emotional swings; unstable relationships; explosive anger; chronic feelings of emptiness; and paranoia and dissociation. Between them, on an hourly basis, they continuously find a way to fuck up my life.

When I say 'a voice in my head', you might be imagining disembodied voices telling me to do this stuff but it's not that. What's so terrifying is that it's *my* voice. The same one that tells me I'm hungry, or I need a wee, or not to take off my trousers in public. That one. It's *that* voice that tells me to kill myself. Which is terrifying, because I *believe* my voice and I think they're *my* ideas. So I've made the decision that some of those ideas, the self-destructive ones, those are the other guy, doing the most scarily accurate impression of me there can be.

I have learnt to survive every day by dissociating from my BPD. I call it Mick, as in Jagger, because in my mind's eye he looks like those gigantic lips in the Rolling Stones' logo. Mick is just a massive mouth that lives in my head and comes up with lots of different reasons for me to kill myself. By doing this, I have learnt to detach myself from the awful things he tells me I am, and the even worse things he tells me to do.

It's exhausting to constantly find a way of differentiating between the things that I'm actually thinking, and the things that he's telling me.

And for most of my life I was unable to do it.

I remember the exact day that my BPD properly woke up inside my head. I was 27 and somebody told me that I had to live with the consequences of the worst thing I'd ever done. (There'll be more about this later.) I now know Mick had been lurking there without me realising for years. I had gone from being in the final three to play Harry Potter at 11 years old, to the youngest British Champion magician in history at 15 years old, to being a regular in a nationwide TV series at 20. But as my life fell apart, and my undiagnosed BPD came to the fore, by the time I was 24 I was a suicidal drug addict. It was a long slow process of recovery.

I'm 34 now, and this year I'll celebrate being ten years clean and seven years sober. I live with the love of my life and have learned to talk openly about my illness.

Three years ago I decided to start speaking about my broken brain in public, because I realised I'd spent my whole life lying about it. I had kept trying to fix myself, but everything I did seemed to make it worse. I had tried various extreme ways of getting away from the person I really was.

I was a drug addict. People told me to stop taking drugs, so I did. I started drinking. People told me to stop drinking, so I did. But it still got worse. I found new things to take. I started trying to kill myself. And people weren't big fans of me doing that, either.

The reason I started talking about my brain in public was because I'd run out of fucking options. I had tried to fix myself by doing everything people had told me to do, but after I'd exhausted all of those suggestions I *still* wanted to kill myself. So I needed to find a way to live with wanting to die.

I needed to find a solution that meant I wasn't the only one who knew what was going on. So, I told my family. I told my friends. I told strangers online. And now I'm telling you.

I had got to a place where I felt like nothing would keep me alive, but telling people, talking about it, has.

But Why Are You Telling Us in a Book, Joe?

I have spent the last three years being absolutely honest and open online about what happens in my head. And I have heard thousands of times that it means other people feel a little more able to be honest and open about what is happening in their heads. I wanted to write a book because it's a place where I can be honest and open in a different way – with more nuance, more detail and more time to explain than a two-minute video. I think that the more honest I am, the bigger a space I open up, the more conversations happen in it. Because of this honesty, I often find myself out of tune with the general public discussion on mental health, where it seems it's OK to open up about mental illness but only the fluffy end of things. Go for a walk, take up a hobby. Fine, tried that, still want to kill myself. Now what? I have full sleeve tattoos to cover up the scars on both my arms. I don't think what was missing was some mindful colouring and remembering to drink more water.

Throughout this book, I really want to guard against cheap narratives of redemption and being fixed. Even the act of writing a book implies that you're out of the shit, and some-where stable, looking back at it. Somewhere at least stable enough to put a typewriter and one of those big piles of blank paper. But the truth is I'm still right there in the shit.

Writing this book has been as chaotic, difficult and fraught as anything I've ever done. What you're reading here had to be dragged into the world, with Mick telling me that every single word, sentence and chapter was shit and would make everyone I love hate me and strangers walk up to me in the street and punch me in the face.

I have written this book to save my own life. Because I had run out of options. I had done everything else and I still thought about killing myself every day. But if there is even the smallest chance that me telling you how I live with me helps you live with you, and opens up a space for you to be more honest about your mental health, it will have been worth it.

If there is a chance that one person is more likely to have a conversation that stops someone killing themself because of anything I've ever done, I have to take it – even though to do this properly I've had to tell you what I've done, and I *really* don't want to do that. Up to now, I'm the only person that's seen my whole life, so I'm the only one that knows quite how much of a twat I've been.

I'm scared. Terrified, really. I'm scared of what you'll think of me, because even though I don't know you, I don't want to disappoint you, and I am *desperate* to be liked by **EVERYBODY AT ALL TIMES.** (Seriously. If I'm in a shop and I think the person on the till doesn't like me, I will spend the rest of that day thinking I've ruined their afternoon, then worrying and wondering about how I could've been a better customer.)

There are things I am writing here that I haven't yet told the most important people in my life and I'm terrified about what will happen when they read them. And I really need you to finish the book if you start it. Because if you stop reading at a certain point, I'm going to look like a complete arsehole.

But if I tell you everything, all that bad stuff won't just belong to me. I've found it easier to live with myself publicly taking the piss out of my illness than I did publicly lying about it. So I figure, a book taking the piss out of my illness – all those printed words – will work even better because I can give them to you and then it's not just mine any more. This is not wisdom handed down from on high.

In showing you what the world looks like to someone who is constantly teetering on the edge of their symptoms, I just hope you'll get something that might help you as you try and understand what's happening in your head, or the head of someone else in your life. (Plus, for you, a happy bonus is that me recounting some of the shit that's happened to me is likely going to be no-strings-attached entertaining.)

One thing I want to make absolutely clear: this is my story. I don't pretend to be an expert and I certainly don't want anyone to view anything in this book as life advice.

My addiction. My life. My suicidal thoughts. My BPD. I can't talk about anyone else; I've only ever been me. I'm not speaking for the BPD community (if that's a thing); that's a responsibility I'm not qualified for. I'm not speaking for others. I can't. I find it hard enough speaking for me.

But by being as honest as I can be, I want to open up a space for you to be honest too, and not worry if it doesn't fit into those neat narratives of fluffy mental health. If nothing else, I hope that this book is a useful record of mistakes to avoid. I hope you'll find something here that makes you feel less alone and more able to talk to someone about what's going on in your head, or think about what's going on in someone else's.

I've spent a big chunk of my adult life trying to work out where the edges of my symptoms end and I begin, the borderline between me and Mick, and at those edges, I think I've come up against some important things that we all feel. There are ten things I hate about me – and nine of them are him.

Ten Things You Should Know about Mick

1. Each one of the nine symptoms of BPD doesn't happen separately, as the different chapters of this book might suggest. They all occur together in one huge churning mass of tangled shit. But I took the position that *One Huge Churning Mass of Tangled Shit I Hate About Me* was a less catchy title.

2. As mentioned, the nine diagnostic criteria are from *The Diagnostic and Statistical Manual of Mental Disorders, Fifth Edition* (which I'm sure we can all agree is the best edition). If you look up BPD on the internet you'll see similar but slightly different descriptions in different places. I am not using a US definition (just) because I am a transatlantic poser, but because it was this list of symptoms I first came across when I was diagnosed and it was this list that I went through with confusion.

3. As I describe my life with Mick/BPD, I'm going to try and remember what it felt like at the time because I feel that it's important to be honest. I only received a diagnosis when I was 27 years old, and started to think of my BPD as Mick when I was 29 years old. But, as

I look back now, I can see him whispering long before I knew how to recognise his voice. So 'now-Joe' will sometimes refer to Mick, even when 'then-Joe' hasn't yet met him properly. If you find it confusing, join the club.

4. Mick. Is. My. Thoughts. I'm going to talk about me and Mick being separate people, but the reality is I don't have an actual conversation happening in my head, and I only think in one voice: mine. Although I know I wouldn't have done the majority of the bad things in my past if I didn't have a broken brain, I still take absolute responsibility for my actions. Mental illness is not an excuse for bad behaviour, but it can be an explanation of sorts. The shit game show I have to play every day is working out whether the thought I just had was one of mine, or one of Mick's. If I win, I get tomorrow. If I lose, literal death. It's like being on *The Chase* if Bradley Walsh had a knife.

5. Mick is something that works for me and I could never and would never suggest it for anybody else. Dissociative states are not encouraged in the mental health community and with good reason, as they're not a healthy mindset to be in. There are a lot of people who I can imagine finding any positive representation of themselves as potentially harmful. I've not said this is a long-term approach for me and I've not said that the dissociation doesn't come with major risks to my wellbeing, like constant suicidal thoughts. It's a trade-off I've decided I can accept at this point but that's only my trade-off to make.

6. Mick is a real thing to me; you just can't see him. I'm not

doing this for attention. I'm not making him up. People have this notion that people like me are pretending to be depressed, which is bollocks. I'm not pretending to be sad; I'm pretending to be OK.

7. BPD doesn't make you mean or angry. I am, by nature, not an arsehole. But I have done many arseholey things. Most people with BPD are inherently kind; I've just got a broken brain combined with trauma and invalidation. A lot of people have the impression that BPD makes people evil, just because those who lash out are the loudest. Well, hi, I'm me, and I don't like hurting people, but it kept happening and I thought I'd never stop. (I have stopped. If you're like me and think you can't stop doing awful things, I've gone from doing seven awful things a week, to no awful things in four years. Please don't stop reading the book.)

8. Mick living in my head is not a choice. Given the opportunity, I would, obviously, decline having a terrorist that tells me to kill myself living in my brain, but here we are. I can't choose how Mick makes me feel, but I can choose what I do while I'm feeling it.

9. Mick can make it really hard to maintain relationships. Because I am so emotionally sensitive, I can often overreact to things that friends or family do or say. This then makes me behave in a way that doesn't help anybody. I don't generally do this to people nowadays, but it still happens inside my head which is, frankly, shit. But years ago it was always unintentionally targeted at the people I love, which was, for want of a better phrase, shit.

10. When I was diagnosed with Mick, I was actually relieved,

because I thought I was the only person in the world that could be this insane, but it turns out there are so many other people like me, they've written books about it. That probably didn't need pointing out given that you're holding one.

A Brief Interlude on Suicide

Writing this book was in many ways a very bad idea. When you have a voice in your head looking for arguments to convince you to kill yourself, going back through the worst things you've done and writing them down is an understandably fraught process.

But I kept going.

Whenever it has been hard reliving the things from my past that make me feel terrible about myself, that make me feel more likely to kill myself, it has been the thought that this book might make a certain sort of conversation a bit more likely to happen.

'Hello, how are you?'

'Fine, how are you?'

That, in the main, is about as far as checking in goes for most of us. An entire society of people pretending to the waiter that the meal was nice.

So much of the problem is that we don't ask, we don't tell, we don't get to a place where we explicitly say to someone not to kill themselves because we don't even do the first bit of the conversation that gets us to that place.

Why don't we talk about this stuff? I reckon a big part is the potential for social awkwardness? What if they think we're weird for oversharing? What if they think we're weird for asking?

What if it's embarrassing?

Well, fuck that.

We need to talk about this stuff. Because as a society we need to get much better at having conversations about suicide *before* someone has done it.

If someone is not quite in that place and it gets a bit awkward, we need to suck it up.

Their life is worth more than our embarrassment.

And if you're reading this and have ever felt like you want to kill yourself or are even feeling like that now:

Wait for a bit.

That's my key to those feelings that make you want to do something that's very hard to undo.

Wait for a bit.

It will never look good on an inspirational poster. Tattooists don't constantly get asked to put 'Wait for a bit' in Chinese characters. But it's been the key for me.

And though I can only tell you what has worked for me, every time I've felt suicidal, I've waited for a bit and the thoughts have died down a little and then I haven't killed myself. We know that it can be the smallest things that prevent a suicide. The train someone planned to jump in front of was cancelled and it was too cold to wait for the next one, so they went home. Such are the little things that can save a life, but the problem is that such are the succession of mundane things that only need to happen once.

Wait for a bit. And while it might not stop you feeling that way again, it will give you an opportunity to find out about other feelings.

If you wait a bit, another feeling *will* come along. I'm not going to pretend it's going to be a good one straight away. But it will be a different one. And if you wait for a bit more, another one might come along, and if you wait long enough, the likelihood of one of them being a better one goes up.

Whereas if you do it. That's it. You won't be around to see the nicer life you think everyone will have without you. You won't get to enjoy not being you. You just won't be. The maths on that is 100 per cent certain. There will never be another feeling.

Imagine all of the people who will ever read this sentence. None of us want you to do it. Every single time someone gets to this part of the book, they don't want you to do it. We would rather have you in the world. Because with you in the world, there's always the chance of something else happening.

I know it's hard to hold on when you feel hopeless. But try and remember the word hopeless doesn't actually mean no hope. It means less hope. You might have less hope than you've had in the past, but you've only got no hope when you're dead, which you're not.

Please.

Wait for a bit.

Chapter One

Unclear Sense of Self

Markedly and persistently unstable self-image or sense of self

You probably think you have a bit of a shifting or unstable sense of self. You hear it all the time. People have a work and home self. They're a totally different person when they're out with the lads. Or they have their talking to the minicab driver or plumber voice, which is different to the way they talk to their boss, which is different again to the way they talk to their nan. Humans mirror each other in all sorts of ways, taking on accents, patterns of speech and behaviour as a way of making other people feel more comfortable.

People shift over time too – the drum and bass DJ at college becomes a corporate lawyer. Or like the kid I knew at drama school who had a voice like Stevie Wonder and could dance like Anton Du Beke and is now blissfully happy selling carpets out of a van.

We are constantly told that an ability to grow, to change ourselves, is good – positive even. But the sort of unclear sense of self I'm talking about here is very different.

It's terrifying.

Imagine being so unsure of who you are that you can't predict what you might do in the future because you've never felt like the same person for long enough to be able to guess. So, planning for the future? Impossible. For as long as I can remember I haven't bothered with long-term planning at all because I've always just assumed I'll be dead by then. The idea of booking a holiday for next year? Insane. Even someone asking me if I want to go for a meal in a fortnight will genuinely panic me. Will I want a pizza? How the fuck do you *know*?! I'll lose sleep over the idea that this is such a simple thing everyone else can do – take all their past experiences and effortlessly fire them forwards in time in a neat person-shaped thing that is them. I have never done a big shop because the thought of knowing what you will need over that amount of time feels impossible.

It also works in reverse, looking back at the past. Every time I feel good, Mick tells me that this is the best I will ever feel and everything is downhill from here. Every time I look at something I've done, it feels as if it was done by someone else. There are weeks of television I am in that I don't remember making and can't understand how I did. It's genuinely someone else. Videos, photos, memories. My past doesn't ever feel like my past, like some stable foundation I can build upon. I can't imagine having done those things because it was someone else.

When I try and think of myself, it's the emotional equivalent of those mirrors you come up to in a funhouse: in this one I'm really tall; I'm all wavy in this one; here I'm two feet tall. I can walk into a room feeling tall and curly, but as soon as I'm in front of people, I'm the two-foot tall me. All these mirror people are sort of me, but the perspectives have fundamentally shifted.

The thing about Mick is that he has the full resources of everything I've ever thought and felt to make me feel like I don't belong in the same room as actual people.

In every room I walk into, I feel like I'm the only person there who's like me. Like we're all at a party with a strict dress code and I'm naked and covered in red paint, but everybody's too polite to bring it up. My body doesn't feel like it's mine. Every move I make feels unnatural and is narrated back to me by a voice in my head. 'You've shifted your arm a bit there, where's the hand going? Seriously, make a decision on the hand. EVERYBODY'S LOOKING AT YOUR HAND.' I can't imagine what life must feel like just . . . walking around. Doing stuff. Getting on with things. I want to stop people and ask them, 'How are you so normal?'

Even though I've put years of effort into learning coping mechanisms to counteract this overwhelming thought process, Mick shares my brain, so he knows what I'm going to think. I'm like a football manager with a tactics board to get me through the day, but he keeps getting to it first and drawing cocks all over it.

I know on one level that my everyday life problems are no more complicated than anyone else's. But they feel like they are. Imagine flat-pack furniture instructions except they are written in hieroglyphics.

Having a consistent sense of self – knowing who you are – is like being a letter with the right address on the front that gets delivered on time to the right place and when the envelope is opened up, there's a letter inside addressed to the person who lives there.

I'm a parcel with the wrong address on it, stuck in customs and nobody is coming to collect me because the name doesn't belong to a real person. And even if someone did open it, instead of a letter inside there'd just be a massive shit.

A Rose by Any Other Name

First things first. My name is not actually Joe Tracini. Bloody confusing that, given it's there in big type on the front cover, but here we are.

My real name is Joe Pasquale Junior. Being a Junior is normally associated with being a famous person, not the child of a famous person. Hands up if you're a massive fan of Sammy Davis or Robert Downey? But if you've got a famous dad who you're named after, and, at some point, you decide you want to have a career in the public eye, you're going to face a decision.

I am the son of the comedian Joe Pasquale (and my mum, Debbie, but that's less confusing name-wise).

I constantly wonder how much of a boring baby you have to be for your parents to have spent nine months thinking of names and then, when you arrive, they look at you and don't see a Geoff, or a Frank, or a Colin, but instead use the only boy's name 100 per cent *already in use*!

To make matters worse, my grandad is called Joe. My grandad's *dad* was called Joe. My grandad's parrot is called Joe-Joe – four Joes, one parrot. (Not the sordid sequel to *2*

Girls, 1 Cup that you think it is. If you know, you know; if you don't, please don't google. I mean it.)

We'll come to the moment Joe Tracini was born, but first I have to set the scene.

So there I am, Joe Pasquale, son of Joe Pasquale, grandson to Joe Pasquale . . . basically if you wanted to signal to someone they were going to have a life spent grappling with their sense of self, this is an excellent way to do that.

I am four years old and I want desperately to be my dad. My very first memory is of Stevie Wonder. It is my fourth birthday. Stevie didn't make a personal appearance or anything . . . I'm not *that* showbiz. Dad used to do a routine about seeing Stevie Wonder in concert where he'd recreate the moment using a puppet and I wanted that puppet so much. So my first memory really is wanting to be my dad on stage.

My dad's act used lots of props and so there was a constant recirculation, as spare props were stored in my room before being called into circulation if the original broke. From my point of view, this led to a thrilling interplay between me, the toys in my room and the adult world. From my dad's – tax-deductible toys!

I was aware from a very early age that Dad did a job other dads didn't do but I didn't see it as something special. He may as well have been a plumber like other kids' dads, the only difference is my dad did his plumbing in a big room with hundreds of people watching him do it. I thought everyone lived like we did.

Growing up, he would often do summer season and I would tag along with him. Aged five I would do a few minutes at the end of the show reciting a comedy recap of the material all the different acts had done that evening. It was a cute little novelty bit.

I can't really remember a time I didn't want to perform, but now I think I still wasn't really distinguishing performing from being Dad, so that's the shape my performances took. I was literally a tiny him.

A big feature of my childhood was that I was mostly around adults and they would treat me like another adult, because I was always acting like one. But I had no hope of understanding what was going on.

For example, one of the guys from a show once sat me down and seriously explained to me that I needed to work out an act for myself if I wanted to get anywhere in this business. 'Start writing your own stuff, Joe.' I was six.

School's Out
Alongside being part of the adult world, there was school.

I was very aware that I was different from other kids from a very early age. In the other world – at work, if you like – I had been treated like an adult from the start. Surrounded by adults, spoken to like an adult, never patronised. At primary school, I noticed that the tall grown-up people there didn't speak to me the way the tall grown-up people at work did. And I wasn't supposed to talk to them like I did at work, either.

So then I tried talking to the other little people at school the way I spoke to the adults at work, and that failed as well.

I had one way of conversing, as an adult to an adult, and that wasn't working. You can get past that if you're good at the things that school life values, like kicking a ball or running or being good at maths or writing. I was good at none of those things and had little interest in them.

So the kids at school made my life awful. And I never told anybody about it, because that's not what you're meant to do. Not telling anyone about this stuff survives to this day, making it hard to bring it up now, and immediately bringing back those feelings of not being believed.

I got on with the dinner ladies. They were grown-ups but, when I spoke to them like an adult, they objected less than the teachers did because they didn't see it as evidence of disrespect. But lunch break was only an hour long. (And even then I knew an act specifically for dinner ladies was too niche.)

I got on better with girls than boys so would gravitate towards them. The boys wouldn't physically harm you when you were with the girls. So the girls would rehearse their Spice Girls routines and I would join in because I like performing and I liked being with the girls because they didn't physically harm you. The downside, however, was that the boys would see me doing Spice Girls dance routines and physically harm me more than usual because I was a boy doing Spice Girls dance routines.

There was no way of winning. I just accepted that, away from the dinner ladies, my school life equalled physical harm, the threat of physical harm and the Spice Girls. (To this day, a Spice Girl song coming on the radio brings me out in a cold sweat.)

If you'd asked me then, I wouldn't have known I was lonely. But looking back now, I absolutely was. At the time, I just thought this was something we all do on our own.

One memory that stands out happened on a no-uniform day when all the kids said they would turn up wearing football kits.

I had no interest in football so didn't own a football kit, but here was an easy-to-read thing that would make me fit in or make me stand out less. I told Mum I needed a football kit, so off to the sports shop we went. The assistant asked which team I supported and I said I didn't, but I liked the colour red, so a Liverpool kit was chosen. 'Kit' is not an understatement. Shirt, shorts, socks, shinpads, shoes, the lot was bought. They even put 'Pasquale' on the back of the shirt. I was over the moon. I loved it.

I was so excited to go to school the next day in my full Liverpool kit. When I got there, all of them were in Chelsea kits. I didn't know football but I knew this was a problem. Four kids in Chelsea kits dragged me over to a big patch of stinging nettles and threw me into them. I tried to get up and was kicked in the chest. I tried again and one boy flipped me over and ground my face into the nettles before they all walked off.

I lay there for a bit. I don't remember getting up or going back to class or anything that happened for the following week after that. I would like to have a time machine to watch what actually happened because my main question is why didn't *something* happen? The fact I have no significant memories of action being taken suggests it wasn't. There's no way it wasn't noticed, after all.

This is a major feeling I associate with growing up: my inability to fit in even when I tried. I understood things were significant but not their context, which meant I'd fail and end up doing the same thing as everyone else but in a different enough way that I just stuck out even more. I knew football kits were important to fit in but didn't think to consider whether the type of football kit mattered. Like noticing that everyone around you drinks some kind of clear liquid and drinking bleach.

Or imagine that you notice how things are connected but not really their causality. Like thinking that umbrellas cause rain or that people drink pints of beer to soothe their throats because they've been loud. I thought wearing the football kit would cause the feeling of belonging I was looking for.

I remember never seeing the red kit again but a blue one turned up. It breaks my heart to think of us all trying our best to work out what offering the gods wanted from us.

Eventually I was moved to a private school, which my parents thought would be a better environment for me. (Spoiler alert: it fucking wasn't.)

I mean, there were fewer nettle-based punishment beatings but that was about it.

Don't get me wrong, I loved the idea of a private school. I get to wear a suit? Brilliant. Ties? Yes, please. I get to carry a briefcase? Don't mind if I do! And if I work extra hard I get a special tie? Where do I sign up?

But the bullying carried on where it had left off from primary school. Different faces, different uniforms but the same routine, only worse. Everyone would join in, except for a short, fat kid named Billy Thompson. I noticed that if

I wasn't around to beat up, Billy would get it instead. There were two of us at the bottom of the pecking order and it was the closest I had to a friend in school because we had the beating up in common. But when I was around, he would be spared the beating up because it was my turn.

One day, I saw a group of kids shoving Billy around from one to another. A kid called Ivan shouted 'Oi, Billy, Joe just called your mum a chicken tikka masala.'

Several things should be noted at this point:

1) I hadn't called his mum anything.
2) Billy was white and so, presumably, was his mum.
3) I have never knowingly used a popular chicken dish as an insult.

I have no idea why 'chicken tikka masala' was picked by Ivan as his invented insult but it worked, because it reminded Billy there was a pecking order and he didn't want to be at the bottom of it any more. He snapped. After sprinting over to me and bundling me to the floor, he jumped up and down on my head nine times, to the point I had a shoe print on the side of my face.

Both our parents were called in. We were punished equally, because I had called his mum a chicken tikka masala. I hadn't, and even if I had I'd still suggest using a kid's head as a trampoline is a disproportionate reaction. The headmaster told me that 'boys will be boys'. (Here, the first 'boys' presumably means 'bullies' and the second means 'cunts'.)

What stuck with me was the deputy headmaster's response, which was the only positive memory I have of that school.

He took me into his office and said, 'You know who you want to be already. Do you have any idea how many kids outside playing will never, ever know who they want to be? If you stay confident in who you want to be, you'll get there quicker, so stick with it.'

I was left wondering why he was the only adult at school who had ever talked to me like this.

I was also left wondering why the person to jump up and down on my head had to be the one who weighed the most?

Doctor, Doctor

On the last day of term, some of the older kids thought it would be fun to lock me in a skip. Eventually, after several hours, someone heard me screaming and came and let me out. But after the initial terror that I wouldn't be found and would spend six weeks in the skip went away, I spent the entire summer break living in dread of going back to school and into the hands of whoever had imprisoned me. I just kept thinking that they would have stored up six weeks of bullying for me, like a battery of malice. So the day before I was due back I told Mum I had a stomach ache. I had a lot of 'stomach aches' as a kid; I was the boy who cried stomach ache.

But this time, I said I really had a stomach ache, honest (I didn't). A sharp, awful one that wasn't going away. Mum decided if it was so bad, I should drop my trousers so she could see my stomach, reasoning that embarrassment would trump a feigned illness. Not a bit of it; I dropped my trousers like I was in a *Carry On* film.

I was wailing in pain (well, pretending to) at this point, so she took me to our GP's office just as it was closing. He examined me and told my mum he needed to have a serious word with her. I was watching all this thinking that things were going well if even the doctor was convinced. He told Mum, 'We need to call an ambulance now. He has appendicitis and it could burst at any moment. If that happens it's really dangerous.' (It wasn't dangerous because there was nothing wrong with me.)

Mum freaked out, as did I. Not at the mention of ambulances and surgery but at the fact I had invented a set of symptoms and somehow managed to replicate appendicitis to perfection. This wasn't a day off school, this was a crying mother, a concerned GP and an ambulance on the way. At that point there was only one thing I could do. Say nothing and have my appendix out.

I was a kid who was so unhappy at school, I had an emergency appendectomy and five weeks of recovery rather than face going back there. I'd rather they take out an appendix that was sat there minding its own business than get locked in another skip.

This was a lie I'd forgotten was a lie until I was 29. My mum still isn't having it. She still believes I had appendicitis because the alternative is just too weird and scary to comprehend. That your kid would volunteer to be needlessly cut open rather than go to school.

You're probably getting the vibe that we've never really been a family that talked about things. That's just how it goes – two people without the equipment to talk about what's going on in their head have kids, and why should that make them better at it? Their parents probably couldn't either, and their parents before them. Right the way back to two people in a cave looking a bit awkward and *really* focusing on the hunting and the gathering.

My mum has always had panic attacks. My dad had one day off work in thirty years and that was because they thought he might die.

Nobody knows the exact balance of genetic and environmental factors that cause some people's brains to work differently to others. And, to be honest, wherever BPD comes from, I'm more interested in where it's going.

My appendicitis was the first time I'd committed to a big lie and it worked. A pattern had been set that would take my entire adult life to break. Like going to a casino for the first time, putting all your life savings down on red and winning. When I got back to school I pursued a life of committing to big lies, mostly in pursuit of a girl I fancied. The two big lies I told her were that I had cancer and that the tape I gave her for Valentine's Day featured a song I had written and performed.

When she played the song, which she thought was brilliant, to her parents, they pointed out that Joe Pasquale Jr didn't in fact write 'All by Myself'. (Ironically, that would be a lie that ensured I was indeed all by myself.) Once she had established I was not, in fact, the songwriter Eric Carmen, she began to suspect I probably didn't have cancer either. My career as a liar didn't simultaneously start a career in thinking through consequences.

The thing is, if the whole world feels like a mysterious and arbitrary set of rules for a game that no one has ever explained to you, then lying feels surprisingly OK. I'd tried being me in primary school and that hadn't worked so I tried lying instead. Lying would come to damage me in my life just as much, if not more, than the bullying ever did, as the lies kept hurting me long after I'd left school. Throughout my life, I have used lies to make who I am feel like the sort of person someone else will want to be around.

All the World's a Stage

The only thing I enjoyed at school was their drama department. Drama was a bit like being on stage with Dad's shows but instead of pretending to be Dad, I could pretend to be lots of other people. It was a kind of lying where everyone knew the rules and clapped you when you were good at it. I had been in a few plays at school and joined the National Youth Music Theatre when I heard that the call had gone out to play Harry Potter. And the NYMT put me forward.

Spoiler alert: I didn't get it.

Which is totally fine. Obviously. I've actually met Daniel Radcliffe subsequently, backstage at a show he was very funny in, and, as you can see in this recreation, we both felt the same crackling tension at this sliding doors moment.

Joe: (smiles sheepishly) Hello.

Harry Potter: (smiles back) Hello.

Joe: You all right?

Harry Potter: Yeah, good, thanks.

Joe: Ah great. (sniffs) Well, see you later.

Harry Potter: Yup.

Absolutely electric. (I was interested to see that he was half an inch shorter than me. So who really is the real winner here?)

The audition was actually quite a stressful thing – there were loads of different readings in front of lots of different people. At one point I realised the nice blonde lady who'd made tea in one of the auditions was J.K. Rowling.

In the end, my parents' tactic of constantly telling me I definitely wouldn't get it turned out to be the right one. (Is there a word for the opposite of pushy parents? Pully parents?)

I was mainly annoyed that I didn't get to be on a Lego. I *really* wanted to be on a Lego.

When I was 13, I was finally withdrawn from school entirely when a boy on the school bus strangled me with my school scarf until I genuinely thought I was going to die.

On the day that it happened, I still didn't tell anybody. History had taught me there was no point anyway. Boys will be boys. I just sat and wondered what I was meant to do now, experiencing a deep awareness of feeling like I, and what had just happened, didn't exist. A sense of unreality and dislocation. Like dissociation in reverse – this had happened in the real world but my brain couldn't accommodate it.

I still completed the day at school. Mum saw the bruises and scratches on my neck when I got home. Her previous advice to stop bullying had been to tell bullies we had a swimming pool. We didn't, but I assume the reasoning was if they thought we did then maybe they'd like me more. The first time I tried it, the bully just punched me in the face. Telling them I had somewhere they could try to drown me never seemed like a good idea, to be honest.

It had been clear for a while that moving schools hadn't really worked. I wasn't learning anything and I still had no friends. I'd stopped having birthday parties at this new school after my first one there. Mum had pulled out all the stops with a massive inflatable bouncy castle / slide / assault course contraption. A lot of kids turned up and enjoyed it immensely without once speaking to me. It was the first time she'd properly seen my 'I'm not happy at school, nobody likes me' interactions played out in front of her. It didn't help that I was her only frame of reference of what a child was meant to be like.

When I told Mum what had happened on the bus, I was told I would never have to go back. I'd already spent my final day as a schoolkid without realising it.

A Kind of Magic

But, luckily, when I wasn't pretending to be a fictional boy wizard, write Celine Dion hits or have life-threatening illnesses, I had been slowly building up a career as a magician for children's parties after realising magic was a thing I both loved and could be good at. (Also, imagine how big the Harry Potter films would have been if the actor playing him could *actually* do magic? That's my last word on the subject.)

(Though it would actually be hard for him to do certain sorts of tricks. Because he's so short.)

Dad had taken me to the Annual Magic Convention in Blackpool for the first time when I was eight and I'd immediately loved it. I would save up my pocket money all year in a big bottle and spend it there. It felt like the right fit for me and, cocky as I was, I looked at the adults performing at the convention, some of whom were a bit shonky, and knew I could be at least as good as them.

Magic is a very special kind of lying. It's a lie you tell that the audience wants you to tell . . . is desperate for you to tell them. Magic gives you a set of rules with which to operate, that allow you to communicate with people and you know if you've done it right. The trick works or doesn't. If you learn a trick, it will always work. You are the person who can do those tricks and you will be that person in the future. The kind of act I wanted to do was one with tricks and patter, in which you're very naturalistic but you're playing a version of yourself.

To me, magicians were the first psychologists in my life. They were the first people I'd been around that really understood how the mind worked. A magician understands a part of your mind that *you're* not aware of.

That's what makes the illusion work. You don't have to see something to control it. You just have to know it's there. It's just like Mick.

When I wasn't being rolled in nettles, I had been practising tricks alone in the conservatory and I had done my first children's party aged ten. For a 12-year-old birthday boy. Which was a bit odd, because for a start whenever any of the kids stood up, they were taller than me. Another odd thing was that my sole experience of other kids at that point was them wanting to kick the shit out of me, and of me being scared of them. (I did eventually do a birthday party for the younger sister of the boy who nearly killed me not long afterwards and over the years often for younger siblings of the kids who'd made my time at school so miserable. In another context I would have been scared, but in a work context I knew the rules; I knew the controlled environment that performing brings, so I could deal with it.) But if they were sat down, with cake somewhere in the vicinity and me doing tricks, I no longer felt afraid of them. I didn't have to worry about being the right person to fit in. I had the tricks and I had the patter – they had their role, I had mine.

Doing children's magic shows while still a child myself was, from the outside, a bit weird but it never felt that way from the inside. Growing up in a supportive performing household, having been a child that always liked performing, it was a given that entertainment would end up being my job. So starting early was like getting a Saturday job or an apprenticeship. Not to mention the draw of hiring Joe Pasquale Jr. It was worth £150 of anyone's money to see Joe Pasquale's son pull things out of a top hat.

Which is not to say that was the only reason. I like to think I wasn't entirely shit at what I did because I put hundreds of hours into not being shit. And apart from the celebrity connection, the other advantage I had over adult children's entertainers is that I wasn't a slightly creepy man in his forties turning up in a van full of sweets and animals.

Before I left, nobody in school ever knew about my job as a children's entertainer but it wasn't as if I had friends at school to talk about it anyway. I shudder to think how much the bullying might have intensified if they had. All of the work I got for local kids came from my sister's schools, which were entirely separate from the schools I'd attended. Looking back, this can't have been by accident, and instead most likely by design.

By the time I was 13 and taken out of school, I was doing it frequently enough that it was naturally assumed this would be my job.

Looking back now, I think the reason I've always had that level of calm on stage is because it's the one time in my life where I feel like I understand all the rules and I have one job and one purpose for existing, which is to make you look at me so I can entertain you. All the other stuff goes away. The risk of me coming to harm is far less on stage than it is anywhere else in life. Where most people would feel terrified, I feel like I'm safe.

In lots of ways, this book is just an extension of this set-up. By reading it, you're sat in the audience, and by writing it, I'm stood on stage and there's an implied agreement between us. As an added bonus, I'm extremely unlikely to start self-harming in front of a packed house in Nuneaton on a Thursday.

I've tried to get what's inside my head out in real life conversations and it never goes well, but this is a context I understand much better.

I was certainly safer when I no longer had to go to school, although once I'd left, ironically I ended up doing more shows in assemblies than I did maths lessons in classrooms before. It also freed up time for me to work on my magic act.

Ladies and Gentlemen, Please Welcome to the Stage, Mr Joe Tracini

After I left school, I had to do a legally required minimum of three hours' schooling a day. A series of home tutors were tried but didn't work out. My cousin, the cleverest man I've ever met, had recently dropped out of university and was drafted to be my tutor. My childhood memories of him, apart from his incredible intelligence, were that he could pick up stuff with his feet as well as he could with his hands and that he smelled like peanut butter. (It's possible he may have been a chimp.)

I got a proper magic tutor too, an amazing guy called Wayne Dobson. Wayne had a primetime TV series and a massive West End theatre show when he was struck down with MS, to the point where he could eventually no longer perform. He used his vast knowledge of magic to develop tricks he would sell at the conventions I attended with Dad.

Wayne had all this knowledge in his brain and he didn't want it to be wasted once his body could no longer make use of it. He told Dad and me that he knew his hands would stop working soon and he wanted to pass on what he knew to somebody else while he still could.

That somebody was to be me. He'd been offered pupils previously whom he'd turned down, but he decided he wanted to teach me. For the first time, someone was seeing me as worthy of time for myself.

Imagine Wayne as Pai Mei in *Kill Bill* and me as Uma Thurman, learning at the master's feet. Only Pai Mei is a bloke from Leicester and Uma Thurman is a short teenage boy with massive glasses.

At one point, when I was 14, I lived with him for a month of intensive, boot camp training as he imparted as much knowledge as he could about magic. I was entirely self-taught at this point so this was my first experience of learning from somebody else. Ten hours a day, seven days a week. Hundreds of hours of video footage to scrutinise, pause, ask questions about. General grounding skills in magic and ten core tricks to build a routine around. I was obsessively crafting a character I could be, scripting things he would say and do. But the thing was, in order for me to be him, I had to be working.

This will become very important, so I want to flag it. This was the first time in my life that I had a consistent sense of a self that worked around other people. A job equals a person. I was like a ventriloquist's dummy who got put back in the box between shows.

By the end of the training, I had a 12-minute competition act and a 45-minute cabaret act prepared. The next thing that needed preparation was my stage name. Between Dad, me and Wayne, we came down to two options with very different connotations. The first was Joe Schmoe, which was actually the early favourite. Had I been Joe Schmoe, I wonder if my onstage persona would have been an everyman, loser character? The other name came from a conversation with my grandfather, who had come over to the UK from Sicily, Italy. His name was Pasquale Giuseppe Tracini. When he filled out his citizenship documents he put all the names in all the wrong boxes. Our family has a long history of not being good with academic stuff like paperwork, it seems. Middle name went first, first went last, last went middle. Giuseppe Tracini Pasquale was his new name and Giuseppe became anglicised to Joe. His kid was christened Joe and . . . well, you know the rest.

I liked the idea of using Tracini, as it was a kind of stepping away from the family name (literally the *one* family name) but still with a connection to my family without stepping away entirely. It had a nice ring to it and sounded a bit magician-y.

Many years later, when sorting through a box of old family documents, I found the birth certificate that would form the basis of my name. Old Pasquale's family name was Tzinia, not Tracini. It turns out Granddad had forgotten what the family name was and in the moment just made a semi-plausible noise. My name is essentially a cough. In attempting to connect to my roots, I just planted the seeds of a brand new tree.

At the age of 15, 'Joe Tracini' won British Junior Magical Champion and the Ken Dodd Comedy Award. That and the fact I came third in the Magic Circle Young Magician of the Year competition combined to mean I was one of the youngest people ever allowed into the Magic Circle. (My third place was the first time anyone had placed without the use of doves, since you ask.)

Ice, Ice, Baby

I'm 15 years old and I'm rolling around in a pool of paint outside a B&Q in Gillingham (insert your own joke about being a messy drunk). I have gone there after an evening of drinking with my colleagues from the ice rink. I have colleagues from the ice rink because I have somehow convinced the management there that I am 21 and got a job there working full time, even though I'm 15. Which isn't easy when you look like you're 12 years old.

A few of us from the college where I was cramming for exams had gone and had a really good time, so I thought, why not stay? Gillingham, Gillingham. (The Anus of Kent.)

I had taken my acting skills and tried to behave how a man in his twenties would behave. Again, I was a kid in an adult world, acting like an adult. Very quickly I was working fourteen hours a day, four days a week. I would wander about, confidently working the chip fryer, or the till, and if people asked me why I was there I would perform the role of a 21-year-old at work and they'd nod. It was a different kind of role, different kind of audience, but the rules were the same.

Playing this character also got me my first ever circle of friends and they spanned a wide age range. Again, this was new for me and something I found I really enjoyed. One guy in particular was from a big family with some siblings my actual age. I hung out with him at the rink and at his family home and this was where I started drinking. I didn't feel as if I was a 15-year-old pretending, I just was a 21-year-old. If you'd asked me, I would probably have thought that this was how everyone felt all the time. I'm not even sure if I knew that everyone wasn't pretending all the time.

It is a rare 15-year-old who drinks sensibly but I had no portion control whatsoever when it came to alcohol and was unable to start without continuing until I was fall-down pissed. Sometimes in some paint.

I can now see I was doing what for many are the normal teenage rite-of-passage things but in an abnormal way because they were done wearing the disguise of a 21-year-old. Like my fake appendix scare (and my real appendectomy scar), I had committed to a big lie and it had worked.

Alongside the big lie were dozens of smaller lies, some of which were fabrications beyond my means to maintain. I did a job presenting on weekend television, did some magic and then went back to work at the rink like nothing had happened.

The thing about lying is that it puts a type of heat in your belly, even when it's a lie you're not attached to. I hadn't put too much detail into the lies I'd been telling, making them easier to negotiate around. Being good at lying is actually helped by an inability to factor in the consequences but if you lie often enough and hard enough, it changes you in a deep way. My lies were laying down dangerous pathways in my brain for later life. Mick wasn't there yet but he would later use lies in a way that felt very familiar.

The lies weren't premeditated. I had no big scheme. They were impulsive. And I never lied with the purpose of hurting others. I was in the moment, I needed to say something and the truth wouldn't cut it, so a lie would come out. It was then my job to work out how to maintain the lie that came into existence in the half second between a question and a dishonest answer.

Here is an example of a lie from the period: that Daniel Radcliffe had only been only signed on for the first three films and owing to him getting on a bit, I would be taking over from the fourth. (Years later, I would bump into someone from this period of my life, who asked me why I had never played Harry Potter and I explained I had been too busy on Broadway.)

This had the benefit of being a lie with breathing space to be disproven so not a consequence I needed to worry about. All the best lies have a bit of truth woven into them so the fact that I could honestly talk about my auditions and still looked like a 12-year-old provided that.

But I'd also lie about what I had for lunch. No benefit, no pay-off, no reason. Just a way of keeping my lying muscle exercised. I can't do anything in moderation. It just filled the gap between me and the person I was lying to that I didn't think would be filled by me *not* lying.

I'm going to try really hard to not make excuses and to own my fuck-ups throughout this book. If you catch me doing it, you have my permission to shout at the pages. I won't hear you, but you might get something out of it. But, looking back, I do wonder if the magnetic pull of lies was partly due to my BPD even then. To someone struggling with the fundamental rules of life, a lie and a truth both look the same from the outside. And for someone struggling with their sense of self, lying about who they are really doesn't help.

Besides, school had shown me that telling the truth about who I was led to beatings and loneliness, so lying seemed to be the logical solution.

When other people my age were finding out who they were by presenting themselves to the world and gauging the response, I was finding out which fictional version of me worked best in any given scenario. Every teenager does that to some degree, taking on the mannerism or attitude of a pop star or actor they like, but not many pretend to be a low-ranking employee in a municipal sports centre.

I loved my months at the ice rink but none of it felt real, because none of it was based on the actual me. Any positive feelings I had about my experience was always undercut by that. But at the time I didn't see another option.

Mum was happy that I was spending time there. But that's because the previous summer I'd lived in a tent in the garden for three months, so by comparison at least I was making friends.

And then, I just left to go to stage school. There was no dramatic unveiling of my dishonesty, no unmasking. The house of cards didn't tumble around my ears, and there were no recriminations from all the people I'd duped. I just left, without even really saying goodbye, and without anything bad happening to me for a year's worth of dishonesty (apart from a formal warning for the evening I drunkenly rode the Zamboni ice machine around the rink).

Somebody, somewhere in the back of my brain made a note: 'honesty hurts; lying works'.

I left my role at the Gillingham Ice Rink to start my studies at the Italia Conti School of Performing Arts. (The irony is not lost on me that I should really have been able to submit my performance in the role of 'Joe from the ice rink' as part of the audition process.)

Stage School Kids
There are basically three ways you can be good at stage school: acting, singing and dancing. And when I went to see the end-of-year show with my parents, it looked like everyone there was very good at all three. Dad pointed out that it was because they had been to the school and I hadn't. If I was that good already, I wouldn't need to go. And Dad was right.

However, I have always danced like someone trying to get a chair through a revolving door and had to have intensive training sessions, just to make it through the entry audition.

Very quickly it became clear that there were two types of people there – the really talented people who tended to be on scholarships. Where the school made the money was by filling up the rest of the intake with people whose parents could afford it. Like me. So in an inverse snobbery from usual social structures, the poor ones look down on the rich ones because it almost certainly meant they were better performers.

I have such happy memories of my time at college. Others have told me that it's the only period of my life that I speak about in wholly positive terms, with no qualifying statements. I moved into the YMCA where the majority of students stayed and shared a double room with a guy called Dave. This wasn't adult supervision, Dave was only 17 himself. But he was very hairy, so he always felt like an adult.

But most of the time, what I remember of that time is that I wasn't aware of myself; I was just existing in the moment, something that had been impossible to do in the largely solitary life I'd led up to that point. Lying was still with me to some extent, the usual dishonesties of life at that age – like getting served underage in pubs and lying about the amount of girls you've done it with – but they felt within the boundaries of normal.

It was also the first time where, aside from home, I wasn't the only person like me in a room. Being a magician wasn't weird in this environment; it was a skill I had alongside the skills other people have, like ballet or juggling. (Just to be clear, juggling is way below magic as a skill and only just above mime.) There are two types of people in the world. – those who perform and those who watch them. After a life spent socialising with audience members who didn't understand performing, now I was socialising with other performers that *did*. Like me, they had a thing, which they liked to do. For the first time, I felt at home. After a life so far spent feeling completely different from my peers, when you suddenly find there's loads of you with something in common, it's a revelation.

I was doing standard, daft, teenage college stuff and I felt uncomplicatedly happy for the first time ever. I enjoyed most of my studies, although dance continued to be a thing I struggled with.

Here is a moment from a dance class with a legendary teacher that sums things up. At one point, she told the rest of the class to stop what they were doing and watch me, telling me, 'Joe, show them what you were just doing.'

I gave it my all, certain that this was the moment my unique talent would finally be recognised.

'Now I know he looks like that and he's doing it wrong but he's giving it a go and I want you to have that energy.'

I hated the feeling of not knowing what I was doing, especially on stage, which had always been my happy place. It wasn't that I didn't want to dance, I did, but I am terrible at not being able to do something perfectly straight away. It's not like magic where you can go away and learn it for hours before anyone sees you. Dance comes naturally to some people and some people are physically built for dancing and I just wasn't one of them. I'm just about built for standing up.

However, I really enjoyed the singing lessons. It was something I knew I could do pretty well as I'd inherited an aptitude from Mum and it was where I felt most at home. Musicals were the thing I loved and thought I could make a career of. I sometimes sing now and, every time I do, I think about the lessons then, even when I'm not trying to sound like a cat or a French revolutionary or Jesus.

And perhaps there is some parallel universe where that's the end of it. A mixed-up kid, who has difficulty fitting in, finds the perfect career for someone who needs to pretend to be someone they're not, pours all of his energy into his professional life and finds a way to be happy.

Unfortunately, what happened next was that I found something even better than pretending to be someone else. I found ways to utterly obliterate who I was. Again. And again. And again.

I'm going to try really hard to guard against trite conclusions in this book. I don't want to lie, or give false neatness. This isn't a simple redemptive story of wisdom earned through hardship. I still have that fundamental vertigo in my sense of who I am. The process of writing this book has been made more difficult by me not having access to the person that I was in the same way as most people do.

But if living with this condition has taught me anything, it's that contained in the terrifying chaos of change is the seed of its solution. Things don't last. However bad they seem, however permanent, if you give change the chance to happen with you in the universe, something else will come along.

If you scream loudly enough, someone will always unlock the skip.

You can get a tattoo of that if you want to.

Chapter Two

Impulsive and Self-destructive Behaviour

Impulsivity in at least two areas that are potentially self-damaging (e.g., spending, sex, substance abuse, reckless driving, binge eating)

What's something you've done that's impulsive? Blown a big hole in your finances by having a really expensive meal? Gone on a last-minute city break? Got an ill-advised tattoo? Gone on a last-minute city break where you spend too much getting drunk at a fancy meal and get an ill-advised tattoo?

I've been to New York five times and every time I've decided to go at most ten minutes before I bought the ticket.

The last time it happened I was sat in the car park at Heathrow having just driven a girl I'd recently met on the panto we were working on to the airport. In my head I was falling head over heels with her. In her head I was a bloke who asked her how she was every morning and had kindly offered to save her a £70 taxi to the airport.

Fuck it, said Mick from the backseat of my brain. *You're already here, so you might as well follow her. Your life will be amazing! It'll be like a film! And in films, whenever people do this kind of thing – it always works!*

It did not work.

What happened was that I spent the entire flight and then taxi ride and then walk across Union Square imagining her delighted face when she saw me, because what woman doesn't want to be accosted by a sweaty man with complimentary peanut breath. When I finally walked up to her, I proudly said, 'I'm here.'

'*Why?*' came her, in retrospect, utterly reasonable reply.

It turns out that a grand romantic gesture, intended to add joy to an otherwise grey world, can also be very creepy in a specific transatlantic stalker way.

The literal definition of impulsive is something done 'without forethought'. And as we've established, I often find it hard to think about myself in the future, as I don't really have a strong sense of who I am at any given moment, so drawing that graph line of me into the future feels impossible. I find it very, *very* difficult to imagine how I'll feel, even if it's obvious, immediately after making an impulsive decision. Even if I've done that exact same thing 20 times before, I'm unable to remember anything I felt at the time until after I've done it again.

Reverse Déjà Vu

I'm a big fan of time-slip movies. You know the ones – *Groundhog Day* or *Fifty First Dates* – where a character is stuck in a loop, endlessly repeating the same period of time. But the crucial thing is that they're conscious of what's happening. Bill Murray learns the patterns (and the piano and ice sculpture), Adam Sandler works out how to be the person he needs to be to get the love of his life.

But imagine those films if the central character couldn't learn and remember. If it was just the first scenes over and over again of them as a fish out of water, never learning the patterns. But worse than that, everyone around them *can* remember – all the love interests, all the comedy sidekicks, all the extras – and can't understand why the hero keeps making the same mistakes over and over again. Someone once said that tragedy is just comedy in slow motion – a man getting hit in the face with a ladder we all know is coming. Most of my life has been like the first third of a high-concept romcom on constant repeat. Slapstick in slow motion.

And what I've come to realise is if a memory has no connotations, no emotions attached to it and no possibility of learning from it, it doesn't disappear but it may as well not be there because what use is it? If you can't learn from the things that happen to you then you will be impulsive.

This is one of the things that I think kills people with BPD. If you're a person who isn't bad, doesn't want to be bad, doesn't intend to do bad things but does them anyway and finds it virtually impossible to explain why, then that disjunction can make you want to kill yourself. You can't reconcile your sense of who you are with all of the available evidence.

So I do the equivalent of going to New York to solve my problems.

But of course I still have problems in New York. Happiness isn't geographical. Wherever I go, *I'm* still there. Even worse, Mick knows this will give him excellent material for afterwards, when I agonise over what I've done in exhaustive detail. And then I do exactly the same thing again.

And it's not just big things like transatlantic travel. I often find I'm impulsive as a way of fixing how I'm feeling that day, or what I've been doing wrong. So if I'm feeling bad, I'll go: 'OK, I'll fix that by doing something that feels like I've made a choice. That'll end well.'

It feeds in to my real struggle with understanding money. I spend money at the same pace I earn it. I struggle to look long-term from how much money I have today, how long it is until I will have more money and how to make the amount of money I have stretch that distance.

Just the other day I bought a coffee machine in John Lewis that was so expensive the guy on the till went and spoke to his manager to make sure the label on it was correct because he couldn't believe coffee machines could cost that much. When his manager confirmed the price was correct I heard him whisper 'fuuuuck' under his breath.

Every single time, if you asked me in the moment, I would be absolutely convinced that the thing that I buy will be the thing that fixes me; one week it's a coffee machine, the next week an iPad, the next a designer footstool. Every time: the last thing wasn't enough, it's the next thing that will work.

I should also point out here that I have frequently made poor long-term decisions relating to drugs and alcohol. You're probably reading that and thinking, 'Yeah, haven't we all.' Which is true, but I'm not talking about having a piss under a cashpoint. Einstein once said (this is the only quote I know, by the way, so enjoy), 'The definition of insanity is repeating the same event over and over again and expecting a different result.' For me, the event was drinking and doing drugs – while I was high or shitfaced, I was aware of the damage I was doing to myself and others. Come the morning, I'd have forgotten. That evening, I'd do the same stuff over and over again.

Each time you're starting from scratch. And, as I was about to discover, for someone with a complicated relationship with their sense of self and not keen on spending a huge amount of time alone with their thoughts, drugs are an excellent alternative.

I am 18 years old and I have just tried cocaine for the first time. I have never tried drugs before. I have never smoked spliffs or taken pills. But this particular night my friends have got some coke and I trust them and trust doing it with them.

We did a few lines through the night and that was pretty much that. Not a terrible disaster nor a dreadful revelation, at the time not even a noteworthy incident. I didn't bother with it again for a long while.

I'm very aware that when people write about taking drugs, however much they might say they don't want to glamorise it, even saying they don't want to glamorise it is a kind of glamour. It's the glamour of unvarnished authenticity. And coke is just the worst drug, isn't it? It's the ultimate poseur drug. The twat with a twat's haircut coming out of the toilet sniffing. It's people chatting self-obsessed shit about themselves whilst spending a food bank's amount of money on a product that is drenched in the blood of poor people at every stage of its production, transportation and dissemination. The profit from it feeds into just about every part of the network of human misery on the planet. But it's ever so moreish.

About eight months later, I began to get into the habit of taking coke with the same person several nights a week. We were hanging around together all the time and coke just became a thing that accompanied that. No pressure on either side, just a thing that naturally started to happen, often of a weeknight and never when I was out socialising.

We'd do a couple of grams each a night, which is a lot if you're not used to taking cocaine. It made him talk at length about everything under the sun, a common reaction to coke. It made me not want to interrupt him but have questions about what he just said. I'd write these questions down to ask later but as the sun rose and the coke session ended, I forgot what all of those questions related to so never got round to asking them. I had a desk drawer full of sheets of paper with very specific questions written down. I don't want to be preachy about drugs. I can absolutely see why people do them. Despite the amount we were taking, despite doing it locked in a room, I still viewed it as just another social activity. Compared to later life, this was probably the healthiest way I took coke. It was even better than booze for pushing me to the edges of myself. I had picked a drug that was very process-heavy. There was a whole set of stage directions for us to follow. Chopping it up, racking out lines, rolling the notes. It wasn't just the chemical effect of the drug, it was the performative aspect of it too. Smokers will often miss having something to do with their hands when they give up. I can now see that a big part of my relationship with cocaine was that it gave me something to do with myself. Somewhere for my body to be with a purpose. With most people, coke makes them confident and talkative; it kind of turns up the volume on them and makes them feel like they're amazing. I was never talkative, it made me want to be quiet, but it made me feel able to spend time with myself in a way I never had been able to before. It gave me somewhere and someone to be.

This went on for years.

Initially I hadn't known to rack up lines of coke; that was someone else's job. Inadvertently, this acted as a form of portion control for me, something we've established I cannot do. This meant it was always a social activity even if it was a social circle of two. A social oval. I never saw our coke nights as a problem or a concern and remember really enjoying them at the time. My friend delivering a six-hour monologue about, say, crisps and me writing follow-up questions to file away in the morning. A bit of paper with 'Cheese and vinegar?' written on it.

Cigarettes and Alcohol

By now I was just about able to drink in a social setting, often even without ending up covered in paint or hijacking an ice plough. Which wasn't to say the type of drink I adopted wasn't weird. I have never drunk pints. My drink of choice in our preferred local was an Amaretto and Baileys topped up with milk. After a couple of those I would get a tray of Creme Egg shots, a speciality of the house. I had strong bones but diabetes was a risk. The tray of eight shots was all for me, not the sharing platter as they're usually bought, and I would guard them carefully as I drank them one by one.

I had been smoking since the ice rink, first of all dipping into the cartons of cigarettes my mum bought in bulk. I had really had to work at smoking, too, because for the longest time I hated it. Mum smoked the ultra diet low-tar cigarettes with the holes in the filter that felt like you were breathing in a foggy afternoon so it took real commitment to pick up the habit. I couldn't buy my own back then because, unlike ice rink managers, newsagents ask for ID to see how old you are. But I threw myself into smoking with real energy.

(Years later this will lead to me hiding how addicted to nicotine I am by decanting 18 mg of vaping liquid into a 4 mg vaping liquid bottle. This is a process that takes about an hour with an eye dropper and ironically is so stressful it makes me really need a cigarette.)

And I had already experienced self-damaging behaviour in other ways too.

The first Christmas at stage school, I had done my first panto that wasn't me tagging along with Dad. Southend, *Snow White*, Little Joe (not a canonical character in *Snow White* but one that had been crowbarred in). Panto was a popular job for stage school students as they're cheap labour and available near Christmas.

I had lived with a family friend and spent a lot of time in my room drinking massive bottles of Bacardi Breezers after I'd done the show. (One of the cast was younger than me, aged 15, and basically shitfaced all the time because nobody wants to ID a dwarf.)

As I started taking more and more coke, I found myself attending fewer classes at stage school. Various teachers and the head teacher tried to tell me that I needed to turn up to things more. But I had – and this was frowned upon – already signed with an agent and said they could look for work for me. I immediately got an audition for a part in a sitcom and then got the part.

My last months there were spent in a farcical process of trying to be in several different places at once without anyone else finding out about the other one. All this involved telling different people different things and keeping up a mental web of lies so I could remember what I had (or hadn't said) to who.

I even scored an audition for another new part while filming the sitcom. I was rehearsing for the show at school at this point. When the producers asked if I could go to Leeds that day to meet with them, with the cockiness of youth I said they would have to come to me because I was busy. Miraculously, they agreed.

I ended up smuggling them in through a back door and hid them in a cupboard where the hats were stored. These were seasoned producers who had been around the block and I set them up in the hat cupboard, making it clear the door had to stay open so I could hear my rehearsal cues. I had to keep one ear on the tannoy for this and kept interrupting my read-through to go and be on stage when needed. And I kept making them hide if anyone needed a hat. They took it entirely in their stride. It took two hours in total and they managed to sneak out again unnoticed. Here, again, that fundamental knot that refused to come untied. Lies, a chemical that takes you out of yourself and it all just seems to work out for me.

The show I was filming was a sitcom for children's TV where all the other child roles had been given to actual children who lived in a chaperoned house. All my life I'd been a kid pretending to be an adult and now I was an adult pretending to be a kid. I didn't take any coke for a while, but, one night at a party, there was a woman who said she was getting some coke in and asked if I wanted any. I very much did. (Post ice rink, I have only ever worked in entertainment, but I assume this is a conversation that happens more naturally in my kind of work environment than, say, the back office of NatWest.)

I bought a few grams but realised that I still had no idea how to rack up lines. I told the woman this and she taught me how it was done. Those ten seconds would prove to be the most pivotal of my entire life to that point. The fact I could now take coke on my own would be a game changer. By the end of that week I was already doing coke almost every night, in my flat, on my own. She'd turned a key in a front door that I'd walked through into a massive house of fuck. This is the difficult thing to explain about how the impulsiveness and self-destructiveness works. Every single time I did a line, it was the same impulsive decision set within the same framework of the same action thousands of times; but it was like things just reset.

For months at a time, I was a person who filmed a kid's sitcom during the day and took industrial amounts of coke alone in his flat of an evening. They kept putting money in my bank every week, so if I emptied it up my nose, by Friday it would be full again. The hours at work turned into drugs. I didn't need much money for anything else because it turns out sitting and watching DVDs in a cocaine stupor whilst eating almost exclusively crisps isn't that expensive. Your major expense is the drugs.

At this point, I was taking up to six grams a night. To give you some perspective, in 2019, a survey found that in Amsterdam three grams of coke were consumed each day per thousand head of population. So I was putting away the same amount as enough Dutch people to fill the Dominion Theatre.

The coke made time go quicker. When I wasn't working I didn't really know how to exist, and just watching TV wasn't enough to fill those long hours, so the coke was like hitting life's fast forward button. I had no skills to be on my own without work or the company of others to fill in the time. Coke suited me as a way of making those hours I couldn't deal with be over quicker, with whatever was on the TV as a nominal focus.

I still socialised of a weekend but coke was never a big part of that. I wouldn't have people round to my flat because it was harder to control when I could be on my own again. I didn't mind visiting other people's flats of a weekend because I could just sneak off home whenever I liked.

My coke habit never impacted my work except that sometimes I would fall asleep in the middle of scenes during parts where I had no lines. At the time it could be laughed off as a joke, a quirky thing I did and a couple of examples even made it onto a blooper reel. And I wasn't very approachable because it's a conversation that nobody wanted to have, to ask if there was anything more going on.

I carried on taking coke in the chaperone house, alone in my room. The massive paranoia I'd felt that first time stuck around as a standard feature whenever I did coke now. What might have been enough to scare other people off for life didn't even slow me down. Once I'd proved to myself it wasn't so awful I would never do coke again, I couldn't use it as a reason to never do coke again. Stopping wasn't an option. Even with added paranoia I still convinced myself I was doing OK.

One night, the chaperone noticed all the lights were on but had no idea why, so my drug habit wasn't discovered. The cleaner did that, finding a load of empty self-seal bags under my bed. My inexperience in doing housework had finally bitten me on the arse in a massive way.

A meeting was called and I immediately confessed to everything. The producers offered me excuses I could've grabbed at – was I having problems at home, was I holding it for somebody else, etc.? – and I said, 'No, I just really like doing drugs.'

I take responsibility for a lot of the things that happen in my life, maybe too much sometimes, but the benefit of doing this is that it's helped me deal with my problems.

The producers just asked me to stop taking drugs and I said yes. I didn't. Of course I didn't. But I said I would. It happened a few days before filming ended and the feeling was like a car with a flat tyre 200 yards from a garage. Let's just get to the end, shall we?

I started filming an adult sitcom in London and moved to a shared flat. I loved doing the show as it filled a lot of needs for me. I was going to be on TV, I knew I was good at this, I was going to work every day and I got to film in front of a live audience, which scratched my theatre itch.

The show centred around five teenagers – two couples and me – who hung out in a shed and told a series of single-entendres. I played a kind of Ali G-esque teen obsessed with sex who was a rapper. I was easily the broadest character on the show and I realised that the only way I could make his dialogue believable was to make him as normal as possible and unaware of what he was like.

Filming in London meant I was meeting new people, one of whom was Phil. Phil was a drug dealer but he was always really nice to me. It wasn't until years later that I realised that Phil was in fact also a pimp. It's a good example of how my adult consumption of drugs in no way related to an adult knowledge of life. It just didn't click at the time that he always had other women in his car alongside what I now realise were their customers . . . I just thought he was a people person. I considered Phil a friend. I liked him. Which was fortunate as I saw him an awful lot due to my now quite large drug habit.

I kept spending whatever money I was earning. Work expanded to fill the space available and so did my drug habit. I was fine, I said to myself, because nothing I was doing was making my world fall apart. There was work me and there was drugs me and there was a tiny, ever-diminishing space between the two that I wanted to try and close completely. It did make my mouth fall apart though. On a rare night out to a house party I rubbed coke into my gums – my preferred method of taking coke in social situations – but it was actually rat poison. Over the next couple of weeks it ate away at a third of my gums with acute necrotising ulcerative gingivitis.

As with any physical ailment, I ignored it until I couldn't any more. The pain was agonising and I was clutching my mouth to relieve the pressure. When I went to an emergency dentist, the damage to my gums was permanent.

In between work, I didn't have enough time for self-reflection even if I thought it was required. And when I wasn't working I stopped taking cocaine, because I had no money to buy cocaine. My rationale was that another job was starting shortly so the cocaine could start again then. This is not what addiction looks like in almost every other case. If you're addicted to coke, you're addicted to coke and your bank balance has no say in the matter. It's not a physical addiction that you can think away but it's an addiction nonetheless.

There was a reason I could stop and start taking cocaine in a way virtually no other cocaine addict can manage, but I wouldn't learn what it was for a very long time.

I'd more or less stopped drinking by this point too. I realised that, while on coke, I could drink indefinitely and it would barely affect me, so what was the point? A wasted effort of self-destruction. My brain could wait out a few weeks of unemployment here and there for when the coke started again. I spent three years living like this.

After the adult's sitcom finished, I was offered a possible role on a soap. I looked down on them a bit and it wasn't ever an ambition, but a job's a job. The producer had seen my TV work and thought he could find a role for me. Even if I didn't want the job, I lost nothing by chatting with him. We did a read-through and some workshops and while they went well, they didn't feel they had a potential role I would be right for.

At this point, for the first time, I had no work lined up. I knew I didn't want to do any more of the kids' sitcom, which was about to be cancelled anyway. The producer for the soap decided that, even if he didn't currently have a role for me, he wanted me to be on the show, so I was signed on a retainer for three months to stop me from taking another job while they worked out who or what I was going to be.

Panto Break

Panto that year was in Croydon. Anyone who's visited Croydon knows that when somebody shouts, 'He's behind you', you don't reply, 'Oh no, he isn't', you run away. (This is a joke. Croydon is a lovely place with excellent transport links and really doesn't deserve its reputation for being rough as a badger's arse.)

Ordinarily I would stay clean while I was doing panto as the schedule is so hectic you don't really have time to find a reliable dealer, arrange to wait for him in a car park for hours, stay up all night getting out of your mind and still have the energy to face a matinee performance of noisy ten-year-olds. Also, talking to a six-foot goose will do nothing to help your come-down paranoia.

But that Christmas was the first time panto and drugs had combined in my life. What didn't help was that there was a bar a short walk away from the theatre that frequently did lock-ins. Clearly, as an addict who wanted to be liked and was increasingly unable to spend time with themselves or anyone else without chemical help, I wasn't going to turn these down to go to my lodgings with a green tea and a good book instead.

One regular at the lock-ins was the person who became my local dealer. Eventually it got to the point where I would get him free tickets to an evening performance so we could arrange the drop-off afterwards. I think he saw the show seven times in total, which when you're a bloke on your own with no kids and look, without wishing to be rude, like a drug dealer, makes you stand out a bit. When you're an addict you're far less subtle about your habit than you think you are and going to the box office for the seventh time to say 'Yeah, my mate really wants to see the show – again' is a good example.

As a result of the late-night lock-ins, the work schedule and the drug use, I wasn't sleeping at all, which in turn didn't help my decision-making processes. It was when I was just finishing up panto that I heard that a friend of a friend had just moved into a new house and was looking for a flatmate.

The Flat Where Souls Go to Die

I want you to imagine a flat. It's in a nice area of a historic city. You know the sort of area: full of artisan cheese shops and coffees that cost the same as a night out in the Wetherspoons a few miles up the road.

It has high ceilings, original features and a coked-up Joe staring at you angrily because he thinks you're talking about him behind his back.

For those first three months in the new flat, I stayed awake, like people in the North Alaskan winter waiting for the sun to start setting again, and did drugs. My new flatmate, Patrick, told me on the day I moved in that it was a 'no judgement' household. I think he probably meant he wasn't going to give me shit for not tidying the kitchen, but I took it to mean something else. I won't say it was like a lightbulb going off in my head, but it was like a door opening that I didn't even realise was there. Patrick always believed you should have a bottle of champagne in the fridge, ready to celebrate the good news that was coming. I applied this rule to cocaine.

By (un)happy accident, I had been introduced to a dealer called John who dealt in high-quality cocaine in high-end amounts. His cocaine was more than twice as strong as what I was used to. You paid a lot more for it but, like its namesake, it was like the difference between supermarket value cola and the real stuff. A sensible approach would be to take less of this higher-grade coke but, because my habit was anything but sensible, I continued to take the same volume despite it being about twice the strength.

There was the very rare regular companion, but most people only came to the flat once, in spite of how good the drugs were. People would come round for a night and never, ever return. The flat had developed a weird, dark energy, despite its grandeur. For some reason, as well as glaring at anyone in the flat, I insisted on the TV having Babestation on in the background all the time. If you don't know what Babestation is, be grateful. It's a TV channel in the upper reaches of your cable TV schedule where bored, semi-nude women wriggle about on a sofa and try to entice viewers to call them on a phone line that charges more than the minimum wage per minute. One day a friend was visiting and asked, not unreasonably, whether I minded turning the channel off. I told him if he didn't like it he could leave, which he promptly did.

The only people who ever came back saw drugs as a challenge. It turns out that the people willing to put up with that environment are a very self-selecting group. I remember someone saying he'd read that Jean-Claude Van Damme once spent £80,000 on coke and, rather than see it as a cautionary tale, this was seen by the room as a goal to aim for, like someone had just mentioned their half marathon time.

Patrick was often away at his girlfriend's house and while I was de facto in charge of the new flat, I let it go to shit. The front room was massive but neither of us were massively focused on furniture – him because he spent a lot of time somewhere else and me because I literally only needed a sofa and a low table. There was a TV but no ashtrays, so people would just use whatever empty drink container was handy. One night early on, a really wasted guest had just started pissing into a mug and I'd had to hold it under them as they got up to walk to the toilet. From that point onwards, the flat always smelt a bit of cocaine urine.

What would quite often happen would be that at some point in the night, someone would have a lucid, sober moment and ask the room what the fuck they were doing. But no one would answer, as they were down in their own furrow. If we'd ever synchronised maybe things would have been different, but instead there would be no answer and they'd join back in.

One night, there were two of us in the room – me and a big, brooding, handsome guy with a really intense energy who I had made friends with by not backing down when he'd done something weird at a party. We decided to swap personalities for a laugh. This would've been more entertaining to an outside observer if we weren't both fixed into our silent, locked loop of drugs. We acted as each other for most of the day but entirely inside our own heads. After many hours, I asked him if he was still doing it too? He nodded and the night carried on in silence. I realise to most people this might not seem like a barrel of laughs but in the grip of addiction, the concept of 'good times' is all relative.

As always, I thought I was getting away with it at work, but when you're filming a scene and you fall asleep while other actors are doing their lines, people notice. In the end they filmed around me and I did my bits of dialogue separately once I'd woken up. It wasn't ideal but things felt like they were still on track. I thought I'd settled into a routine that would last for ever. I had a reliable coke dealer, a regular income and no threat that anyone would upset the cocaine cart.

It was then that the closest thing I had to a regular companion told me he was giving up coke. He was sat on the sofa, days into his latest binge, wrapped in a duvet and I proposed we got back on it.

'No, fuck it,' he said. 'I'm done.'

At the time I convinced myself that he just meant he couldn't be bothered travelling all the way to London when he had important duvet-wrapped sofa sitting to be getting on with.

His decision to quit was my first inkling that what I was doing was killing me. A couple of weeks later I realised that there were no more guests coming around so I was using with no outside influences. Excessive though my habit had been for a while, taking drugs with other people still kept some semblance of the existence of a handbrake even if the car was doing 80 mph up the wrong lane of the motorway.

I went from six grams a day to eight grams a day, almost immediately. And I knew I couldn't stop. Hard as it is to believe, the idea of stopping never even occurred to me. I didn't think I had to stop, so why wonder whether I could? Everything was fine. But now I saw that stopping was not only an option but a desirable one and it forced me to look in the mirror and admit I couldn't stop. Seeing him when he was in the flat, getting back to a normal life, was a reminder of this.

Despite this, the part of my brain that was still sane knew this couldn't end well. It was the first consideration of my own death. I'd had a couple of sick days at work that were drug-related but this was something altogether different. I was dying. Patrick could see this but this wasn't his fight. In fairness, anyone could probably see I was dying. I hadn't eaten properly in months and I was emaciated. I must have smelled dreadful. Everything about me screamed of sickness. I made excuses to my family that I couldn't see them because I was so busy at work, but it was really because I knew that they'd recognise that something was wrong.

I've since spoken to people who knew me at this stage who said, 'Oh yeah, we all kind of assumed you were going to die', which shows how apparent my addiction must have been to everyone but me. By the end of June, even I knew

I was in serious trouble. The problem was, I didn't care. My brain told me I'd been this way for years and hadn't died yet, so what did I expect to do about it?

What I did initially do about it was everything but address the problem itself. I consulted a nutritionist to see if I had a glucose deficiency. I had allergy tests to see if it was a problem with the food I wasn't eating. When I collapsed at work during a dance routine and they called an ambulance, I told the paramedic I might have diabetes.

I also looked at non-medical solutions to the problem that was staring me in the face. I used to like Scalextric, so I bought a kit. It was the only vehicle it was safe for me to drive at that point. I liked Playmobil as a kid so I bought £700-worth of it. 'When I was a kid, I wasn't like this and when I was a kid I had a Playmobil. Maybe the two were connected?' It was the football kits all over again.

Then an Xbox became the solution. It came with a Spider-Man game but I was so incapacitated at this point I could barely move my hands to operate it. Spider-Man 'doing whatever a spider can' with me at the controls consisted of running in a circle for hours at a time.

Patrick was spending more time at home by now, to keep an eye on me. He'd sit behind me quietly, making sure I was as OK as I could manage at that point. After several hours of making Spider-Man pirouette on the Xbox (a 'non-medical solution', along with Scalextric and £700 of Playmobil), he said something in a weird voice. I turned around and it was a friend from work who Patrick had asked to come and watch me because he'd needed to go out and I couldn't be on my own. I hadn't even noticed the changeover.

On one level I knew I was dying and knew I needed help but if the way to make that happen was for my family to find out, I chose death.

A week later, I was in rehab.

Here we are in the voiceover bit. The bit where we draw this chapter together to form a neat lesson. Like when Sarah Jessica Parker finishes the article.

Those cocaine years were *miserable* but one of the big things I have come to realise is that many of my destructive behaviours, the drugs and drinking and lying, were really just different routes to that feeling of oblivion that stemmed from wanting to minimise the amount of time I had to spend on my own, with me. But I'm aware that no matter how many times I say it, you won't know what being in my head is like. All you'll likely be left with is a portrait of a stupid, selfish bloke snorting his immense good fortune away. The thing is that I picked the wrong drug. I like sleeping, eating and laughing. If I was going to get into a drug it should probably have been weed. But I chose the death powder, and instead of getting nice evenings and a good rest all I did was spend a fortune on being with myself for twice as long as I had to be in the first place. I ended up hating being around me more because I was around me so much.

Just like with magic, practice made perfect, and the more time I spent with me, the better I got at hating myself.

It's only in the last couple of years with enough time under my belt of not having done anything awful, that I can truly say, 'You weren't awful today.' And even if I was, I *tried* not to be. Some days, trying is enough. You might not hate yourself, and if so this will sound like the lowest possible bar to hurdle. But ask anyone with a highly developed sense of self-loathing and they'll tell you what a challenge it is. No matter how many nice things I do, and for how long I do them, I always remember all the bad things I've done in my life.

I've been reliably informed that I've done more good things than bad things in my life (not including those eight years; those eight years were shit. But collectively I've been not a prick for more time than I've been one). But I never remember those good deeds, because I only ever feel the bad ones.

Where are the joins between my BPD, my addiction and me? (I don't know why I'm asking you.) I did have an addiction and I am still an addict. I know I can never start doing drugs again, because I know I won't stop. I feel like something fundamental about me has changed, but I know that, from the outside, I'm the same Joe, behaving differently now, but I appear to be the same person.

I know for a fact that there are many people for whom the Joe staring at them, glowing in the light from Babestation, is as much as they will ever need to know. And I don't blame them. But I have to believe that if I stay in the world and give myself the chance to be, I can be more than that – more than that selection of my words and actions, and with enough time and enough different words and different actions I can dilute that Joe until they are a small part of the whole.

Like arsehole-flavoured Ribena.

A Brief Interlude – Joe's Rehab Diary

28 Days Of Me

Hello. This is Joe now. What follows is the diary that about-to-be 24-year-old Joe wrote during his time in rehab. I include it here, lightly edited for repetition, to show you what I was working with.

July 4th, 2012.

Independence Day.

Quite fitting for the day to check into rehab, to rehabilitate myself from a serious cocaine addiction.

I'm a fucking rock star.

Four days awake, three bottles of whiskey, two bottles of Sambuca and a pile of coke the size of a partridge in a pear tree got me here. More coke than I'd care to admit. Nearly £1,200-worth. Oh look, I admitted it. Smooth.

Dickhead brought me here. 'Dickhead' being the nickname for my flatmate, the kindest most loyal friend you could hope for. A dickhead nonetheless. Once we'd decided to come here, I'd packed a bag, necked a whiskey and coke while nobody was looking, and had one final line of coke. Just one more for the road.

I pleaded with Dickhead on the drive here to turn the car around. I told him I could sort this on my own. I knew it was a lie even as I said it. So did Dickhead, which is why he said nothing and kept driving.

It's all a bit chaotic when I arrive, with me providing most of the chaos. There's nurses and doctors and paperwork and questions (them) and crying (me) and at one point a takeaway I ordered (Domino's).

Delivery bloke: You OK, mate?

Me: I'm in rehab, the fuck do you think?

(Actual me being all British and polite: Yeah, cheers.)

I meet a few of the inmates including Simon, who took ten minutes to describe the game of pool he'd just played. 'I'm on quite a lot of drugs,' he finished, by way of explanation.

So was I, mate.

DAY ONE

My first night's sleep in a bed, rather than passed out on the couch, for seven months. A 9 a.m. chat with a doctor asking non-judgemental judgemental questions, then more sleep until lunch. I'm told off for putting salt on my food as it's bad for me. I'm too tired to comment on the irony.

Slept until 7 p.m. I've averaged about two hours a day since Christmas so this is like me binge-sleeping. More chats with the inmates, including Simon again. I've already noticed anyone talking to Simon has the expression you have when somebody you knew from school spots you in Tesco and bends your ear for ages while your Viennetta quietly melts in your trolley.

The other guy I've chatted to is Louis. He's quiet but seems nice and supportive.

Dickhead popped over a bit later, dropped some stuff off, ate my food, was rude and inappropriate then left. It genuinely made my day.

I want to be here. It's the only place I can be. I like it here, and I simply cannot wait until I'm ready to not be here any more. In the meantime, I'm looking forward to tomorrow.

DAY TWO

Yeah, that was a bit optimistic. Today has not been a good day. I say 'today' but I slept until 4 p.m. (developing a bit of a sleep habit, might have to watch that) and when I woke it hit me like a lorry where I am. In a place where nurses check every half hour to see if you're dead and the only people who don't look like they're about to start screaming are the ones currently screaming.

I stay in my room mostly. I'm not very social as I don't know what to say when I don't have a script telling me how to be a normal human. When you casually ask people here how they are, they actually tell you. 'I'm worse than you, so fuck off. Did you steal my cheese?' That sort of thing. I've been telling people I'm fine for too long when I've been very not-fine, so maybe I need to follow their example. Apart from the cheese bit. I don't even like cheese.

Louis tells me he's only 17 and has a nurse stationed outside his room rather than the half-hour checks. He doesn't know why he does the things he does that hurt him, any more than I do when I do them. I like how honest he is about himself and I notice the contrast with how much I've lied about myself. I want him to feel better and I want to try and help with that.

I also want the nurses to stop injecting vitamins into my arse because it really hurts.

DAY THREE

A nothing day. I'm already beyond sadness. It's like a terrible bank holiday in Margate with your nan where she never left the turd-brown hotel room, to pick an example entirely at random. I desperately want to end this and we haven't even started yet.

DAY FOUR

Still hiding in my room, still sleeping. The staff want me to mingle with the inmates, like your mum telling you to go outside and play when it's sunny. Respectfully, piss off. My whole life has been talking at work and people outside of work trying to talk to me. Therapy starts tomorrow, more talking. Just let me sit here and work out how my head works when I'm on my own and I'm not filling it with drugs, please.

One reason to leave is the attractive lady nurse in our midst who gives out the meds. She seems lovely, and back home, we might have chatted and got along, but in here, I'm room 21, 25 mg diazepam, 15 mg Librium twice daily, so I think I'll probably leave it.

Really having to keep my head down at visiting hours. I'm not playing the reclusive Hollywood star, I don't think a lot of myself or anything, but I'm trying to keep this out of the press for my family's sake. They and my friends are being incredible. Calling, texting, visiting. It's really helping. It counters the loneliness and they bring crisps. Potatoes don't feature in most self-help books but they make me happy.

The doctors now think I'm an alcoholic as well as a drug addict. I don't think I am but that's just what an alcoholic would say, I suppose.

DAY FIVE

My main 'homework' following today's group therapy is that I have to write a 30-minute presentation of my life with drugs. Didn't start it as I've come over incredibly unwell. I can't hold down food and feel dreadful. I have an odd worry that I'm going to die. I hope my body isn't so bruised that it can't cope with another illness.

DAY SIX

Still feel rotten so missed today's therapy, which I honestly wanted to attend.

But somebody from work turned up to say hello and brought McDonald's, so swings and roundabouts. Moved to a bigger room that's less like a turd-brown hotel in Margate.

We're on the up, people.

DAY SEVEN

One week since I told Dickhead I needed to get better. It's whizzed by but also feels like years ago.

The hardest bit is seeing the effect on my sister. Mum and Dad knew I was going downhill but my sister completely broke down when I told her on the phone. Hearing her sobbing, hearing the phone drop, hearing my nan telling her not to run out of the house, broke whatever parts of me were still intact.

Still too ill for classes. Cocaine's not physically addictive but my extreme abuse of it, combined with eating one meal a week for months, caused my body to start shutting down. The doctor estimates if I hadn't admitted myself on Wednesday, I'd have gone into liver failure by Friday. What's more terrifying is that I don't have much emotion attached to that information.

I'm well enough to attend my first Cocaine Anonymous meeting this evening. Yes, cocaine is so terrible it has its own sub-meeting. I turned up late to a group of 50 people sharing experiences that were all too familiar.

Because I arrived late I had to speak last. Top of the bill on my first meeting. Still managed to get some laughs, though, so a pretty decent gig considering the circumstances. Ended the night feeling as positive as I have since I got here. I'm not alone. Bring on tomorrow.

DAY EIGHT

Group session. I strongly feel I'm not the same as some of these people. I'm listening and learning but I'm not on board with the helplessness and the surrendering to a higher power. That may change, I'm open to suggestions, but it just doesn't feel like me.

I do feel more alive than I have in years, though. Alive enough to imagine sexy times with one of my nurses and how disappointed she'd be.

Dickhead came over, had a shower, broke the curtain off the rail, left it on the floor then went home. My manager discussed a BBC script I'm wanted for and they're letting me out to go to the meeting, which is amazing.

And it's the first day in months I've stayed awake all day. I'll take that as a win.

DAY NINE

No, sorry. I can't do this 'higher power' business.

They're keen to point out they don't mean 'god' when they say 'higher power', it just means 'higher power' but 'god' is quicker than 'higher power' so let's just say 'god', shall we? Give yourself over to not-god we're calling god.

I'm powerless against my addiction, apparently. Self-help based around the word 'can't'. Oh, great. And apparently there's no other solution but theirs, which is financially convenient, too.

Their many books and DVDs for sale say I might be unhappy and disbelieving about all this and I am, because it's bollocks. Don't tell me it's not god but call it god. Don't tell me a higher power got me here, rather than doing something to help me. I got me here. Me.

I'm trying to keep an open mind, as I need this but surely there's other ways to do it? Google seems to think so because when I searched 'Are the 12 steps a cult?' I got 27.6m results.

I'm not knocking religion. If that gets you through the day, brilliant. People need to believe in something. But if you tell me that if I don't believe in a god – sorry, higher power – I'm doomed to be an addict, I'm calling bullshit.

I need help. I need direction. I need support – from professionals and loved ones. But above all I need me. Not Jesus, because he wasn't the one chopping up lines, I was. And I will do this. Fuck these clowns.

DAY TEN

Tired. Getting harder not to dismiss 50 per cent of this as cult nonsense but I'm trying. This is the longest I've gone without cocaine for a year. They say days 10–13 are the hardest when kicking cocaine. Goodnight, day ten.

DAY TWELVE

Another low start to the day. Then I read out my 'drugs story' to the group and that low feeling went away. I was quite emotional by the end, which I'd not expected. Talking to people helps, it seems. Somebody should recommend that.

Cheered up further with news I'm allowed out for a meal with my family. Lucky me.

One blot on my mood is the new arrival, a funereal-looking guy with depression who's spent all day cackhandedly playing *Adagio in C Minor* on the organ they have in the communal room, which looks like the kind you get in a nursing home that ends up on the news.

DAY FOURTEEN

A family visit that started with them shocked at the state of me, even though I've spent two weeks eating regular meals. They were also pretty pissed off after a seven-hour traffic-buggered trip to get here. The visit ended with me running after their car doing full-body sobs, waving my arms about and shouting 'NO! NOT YET!' The car screeched to a halt and I got to hug my mum before they finally had to leave.

The day ended with me having to tell the staff that Bog Eye Phil, who's here waiting for an NHS psychiatric ward, had wandered off into the night. Their look of panic reminded me that I don't have a lock on my bedroom door.

Shit.

DAY FIFTEEN

My twenty-fourth birthday.

In rehab.

My Rehabirthday.

I wasn't ready for how hard today would be. Cards from my family, even a card from the inmates and staff, a realisation that if I hadn't come here two weeks ago I'd be dead by now. Stuff like that can make the strongest of people cry. Which, y'know.

I always use my birthday as a benchmark, a time to wonder where I'll be next year. This is the first where I'm 100 per cent certain it'll be a better place, I'll be alive and I'm lucky for each day between now and then. I couldn't ask for anything more.

Maybe a blow job, but this is fine.

DAY SIXTEEN

A tough day in therapy, where we talked about trust and I admitted to my reservations about the programme and they said that was my addict talking.

I disagreed but, as someone else in group said, 'My thinking got me put into a psychiatric ward', so what do I know?

I tried to help a guy who's been struggling recently. Just sitting with him to pull him through. He punched me in the face. A tough day outside of therapy, too.

DAY NINETEEN

Went for a BBC script read-through yesterday in London. Because I'm still in treatment, I had to book a hotel with Mum in an adjoining room and she kept popping in to check up on me/offer me crisps. It's not quite *Scarface*.

The read-through went brilliantly. Currently on the way back to the shithole, doing written work for step one of the 12 steps:

'Do you accept that you have lost control of your addiction, or do you believe you could control your intake or behaviours?'

I KNOW I can do it my way. So, I've been honest. Why lie to keep 'them' happy? I looked my broken-hearted little sister in the eye and swore to her I'd never do it again. I don't need the 12 steps, I've got her.

I'm sure they'll understand.

DAY TWENTY

I told the group my views on step one and my views on being powerless.

The second part is reading out letters from family, where they say what your addiction has done to them, to the group. Utterly heartbreaking. The last thing I said, while crying, was that the 12 steps are not for me, and I might not have got step one, but I definitely have got something else that will work.

The group and the therapists normally spring to life to defend their beloved system, but this time, it was different. They were all silent.

Eventually, Louis looked me in the eye and said, 'I believe you.' One by one, so did everybody else. It was touching, like something out of a really corny film.

They're right to believe me though. I'm telling the truth.

Sleep disturbed by somebody setting off the emergency alarm. I hope they're OK.

DAY TWENTY-ONE

Louis tried to kill himself last night. He snuck a plate into his room from the canteen, smashed it quietly in his duvet, and cut down the centre of his forearms in the bath.

If I was someone that prayed, I'd pray for him. For now though I'll just keep him in my thoughts.

That's enough for one day.

DAY TWENTY-THREE

Today, I got a phone call from work. It was to tell me the days I'm in next week.

NEXT WEEK.

I'm in WORK NEXT WEEK.

I'm alive. I've got a job. I've got my friends, and I've got my family.

Amazing. I was so happy when I put the phone down I cried.

I think that's the first time I've ever cried because I was happy.

DAY TWENTY-SIX

Just 'done' my steps 2 and 3. These steps are about admitting that you are powerless, and handing over responsibility to something greater than yourself.

Fuck that.

I was completely honest, and, even though the terrorists – sorry – therapists can't say it directly, they know I'm right. I can't wait to get out to prove that my way works. That you don't have to have a complete lifestyle change to change. You just have to change. By marrying some of their suggestions with my unshakeable determination to be the best that I can be, I WILL succeed.

DAY TWENTY-SEVEN

Penultimate day. What a fucking journey. Tonight I'll sleep knowing I'll never, ever come back here.

I cannot believe I've made it. I came confused, hating myself, and I'm leaving knowing what I want, and liking myself. You can't put a price on that.

Well, you can. £16,000.

DAY TWENTY-EIGHT

Last day. LAST FUCKING DAY.

Had to get a taxi home cos Dickhead was working. The journey back was incredible. I put my iPod on and poked my head out the window like a dog, and I felt free.

And now, I'm home. Back where it all happened. I've been so excited about this that I haven't prepared for this to be anything other than great. And it's not.

It's terrifying. I'm not scared of doing drugs, that's never happening again. I think I'm scared of living, the real me has only come out while I've been institutionalised. Never in the real world though.

Fuck.

This? This, is going to be interesting . . .

Hello, this is now Joe again. Just so you know, I drank that night.

Chapter Three

Fear of Abandonment

Frantic efforts to avoid real or imagined abandonment

She was gone for 90 seconds, she went to buy a carrot and some hummus. She told me, 'I'm just nipping out to buy a carrot and some hummus.' I can SEE THE SHOP out of the window, but as she walked out, this is what happened in my head as the door closed behind her. 'She doesn't love you. That's it. She's never coming back. You're not enough. She hates you, of course she hates you, everybody hates you. The only reason she's not left you already is because she's scared that if she does, you'll kill yourself for attention. Is that a fly or a spider on the window? Course it's not a spider, it's got wings. You're worthless, kill yourself. Shit, if there's a fly you might have mice – did you leave that banana out? You're not enough for her, she's ashamed to be around you. No, that's too big to be a fly. Might be a bee? She's on the phone to her ex, she's still in love with him and she's not even at the shop, she's just hiding behind the bins telling him how much she wishes she was with him not you, because you're disgusting. It can't be a bee, of course it can't be a bee, it's February. What kind of an idiot sees bees in winter? You should kill yourself. Also, why are a bee's knees so good?

I'm not contesting it, but I've never seen a bee's knees and if out of all the knees a bee's knees are the best knees, I need to see at least one set of bee's knee's. Not even a pair actually, just one. I need to see a minimum of one bee knee as a frame of reference. Without knowledge of what a bee knee looks like I'm not in a position to use bee's knees as a benchmark for where to set the bar on knee quality. This is why you're definitely going to die alone. Oh wait, she's back. Never mind.'

Fear of abandonment is an interesting symptom. Because being actually abandoned is definitely something to be rationally afraid of. My dictionary defines abandon as 'to leave a person, place or thing, usually for ever'. And gives the examples: 'We had to abandon the car'; 'By the time the rebel troops arrived, the village had already been abandoned'; 'As a baby he was abandoned by his mother'; and 'We were sinking fast and the captain gave the order to abandon ship.' Notice that in none of these examples do you want to be the thing left behind and in none of these examples does it sound like the people doing the abandoning are having a particularly nice time. You don't abandon the last slice of a really nice pizza because you're comfortably full. There's a frantic, urgent, forced quality to abandonment that never reflects well on a situation.

So actual abandonment: definitely something to fear. But *The Diagnostic and Statistical Manual of Mental Disorders* describes this symptom of BPD as 'frantic efforts to avoid real *or imagined* abandonment' and this is key because the abandonment I'm scared of IS NEVER HAPPENING. Ironically the main reason I'm likely to be abandoned is because I've kept telling someone who isn't leaving me that they're going to.

Because, however close a relationship, at some point, they are going to be in a different room to you. And at that point, the trouble starts. It's not sustainable that every time they go to the toilet, I'm imagining them climbing out the window so they can finally be free of me. I have to refrain from checking in with messages pretty much constantly. It's an especially tricky one because, you know who else wants to know where their romantic partners are all the time? Creepy controlling guys. At a general level, culture tells us that a constant need for reassurance is the opposite of cool. Do you remember that feeling from when you were a kid of needing your parents to look at you while you were doing something but not being able to explain why? Now imagine that fear when the future is a chaotic and unpredictable wasteland, you hate yourself all of the time, find it hard to judge social interaction and are intensely paranoid. The other morning I started crying because I thought my girlfriend was ignoring me. She was brushing her fucking teeth.

This irrational fear of everyone I care about leaving is a background hum to my whole life. Mick tries to convince me that everyone is pretending to like me. Sometimes he says it's because I've told them I might kill myself and they're only being nice to me so when it happens it isn't on them. The only way I can be sure, he says, is to actually kill myself. Then we'll know.

Good plan Mick, you absolute wanker.

For me, this fear of being abandoned is especially intense because I've always felt that if nobody else is in the room with me, I cease to exist. (Or do I? I'm Schrödinger's Twat.) I just have never really developed the life skills that tell me how to be me when nobody else is around. If I'm with somebody, I have a reason to exist, because they're there and I have to do the things expected of me as a human when I'm in the company of others.

It's like how babies have no object permanence (I didn't know what that meant originally either, I googled it). When you play peekaboo with them, your genuinely disappear from the universe and they're delighted when you return. I have always felt I have no function without a person present, to the point I have stopped existing in a full sense. On my own, I had no idea what to do with the time between when the last person left and when the next person arrived. I just sat in silence and waited. I am the human equivalent of when a tree falls in the forest, does it make a sound. For most of my adult life, the only pastime I had when someone left was waiting until somebody else arrived.

I film myself at home these days for various reasons – rehearsing, sketches, etc – and sometimes forget I've left the camera on. I've watched it back and frankly, with nobody around and nothing to do, I'm terrifying. It's so uncomfortable to watch. It's like I'm possessed. Quick, animated movements accompanied with incoherent sleep-talk mumbles while I listen to the voice-thoughts in my head. Like a glitching android. I'm aware that I don't do this in the company of others and I'm aware it must take a lot of energy for me to maintain not doing this. Energy I stop expending once everyone leaves. Like a *Doctor Who* alien, once I'm alone I can unzip the human costume I wear – so you think I'm like you – and whatever I am underneath comes out.

So to recap: terrible pathological fear of being left on my own at the best of times.

I am 24 years old and I am on my own. I am on my own in the kitchen, celebrating putting my destructive and addictive relationship with cocaine and alcohol behind me by opening the bottle of champagne we keep in the fridge for special occasions.

Patrick was away working and the only other regular visitor I could have called to come over for company at that point was a drug dealer, which I figured probably wasn't a great idea.

However much I'd thought about my life sober while I was in rehab, I had put zero thought into what I would actually do to practically to fill my sober days. This is something they are very aware of and they put a lot of time into coming up with plans of how you'll keep occupied so that 'do a load of drugs' isn't a viable option. They know that, for an addict, you're only ever one slip from picking right back up where you left off. The problem was that I had convinced them (through repeatedly lying in exhaustive detail) that I had a busy and varied schedule full of work, friends, family and more that would be my connection to real life and part of my safety net. It's a shame the Oscars don't have a category for 'Most Convincing Drug Addict Scamming Healthcare Professionals with their best interests at heart' category because I think I might have had a chance at a nomination. It was such a convincing performance I even convinced myself. Here, of course, my previous notable work as 'boy with appendicitis' and '21-year-old ice rink employee' stood me in good stead. Though I wasn't unique – rehab has a 22 per cent success rate – looking back, this meant I was especially at risk.

To give you some sense of the scale of the problem: here is what my day looked like by the time I went into rehab.

Timetable of a Day on Drugs

- 7.30 a.m. – Alarm. Wake up on the couch in the front room. Never the bed. Start smoking.
- 8.00 a.m. – Get in the car, drive 10 minutes to work. Still smoking, fourth cigarette is lit in the car.
- 8.10 a.m. – Go to dressing room to get into costume and make-up. Look at the script for the first time. Regardless of how much work I had to do, I would always read the scene for the first time just before I filmed it. I thought the less time I gave myself to learn it, the more unlikely it was that I'd forget it. Drugs were really affecting my long- and short-term memory, and I had to factor that in to line learning.
- 8.25 a.m. – Breakfast, which consisted of two miniature Milky Way chocolate bars. This would be my only meal.
- 8.30 a.m. – On set to film one scene. Rehearsing and filming takes three hours.
- 11.15 a.m. – Still filming, but text John my dealer to let him know I'd be at his house in 30 minutes to pick up eight grams.

- 11.30 a.m. – Wrap the scene, get out of costume and run to the car.
- 11.45 a.m. – Stop at the cash point, withdraw £500. Depending on the quality of coke John had in, a gram would cost between £100 and £140. The £500 wouldn't cover the cost of the drugs I was buying on the day, and I'd technically be paying off the last lot of drugs I'd bought, because I was always in arrears.
- 11.50 a.m. – Trade with John, have a bit of small talk with his wife and daughter, drive back to the flat.
- 12 p.m. – Prep time. Two things are going to happen in the five to ten minutes after I take my first line: I'm going to want to 'watch' Babestation; and I'm going to be paranoid that people are coming to either kill or arrest me. They're really great things to associate with each other, and I'm certain aren't a factor in my ongoing problematic relationship with sex. I know where my terror points are (the places I'm going to be staring at, thinking the people are gonna come in to take me) so I start to barricade myself in. I put towels under the bottom of every door, pushing tables over them so they couldn't be opened. I get gaffer tape, and stick all of the curtains to the wall, all along the sides, the top, the floor, so no light could get in. This all takes about an hour.
- 1 p.m. – Write a text to John asking for more drugs, probably another four grams, because I know by the time I run out I'm going to be incapable of seeing the phone or moving my hands, so I set the text up so all I have to do is press send. Then I rack up the first line of the day,

which would always be a full gram, about the size of a thick eyeliner pencil. I'd cut some plastic straws in half to use instead of rolled up banknotes. I always thought it was unhygienic to put money in my nose because I didn't know whose hands had been on it. Absolutely nailing my priorities there.

- 1.05 p.m. – Do the line, and it starts. Babestation on, and everything I'd tried to prevent kicks in. In spite of the tape, I manage to find a crack in the curtains to be absorbed by, I start to hear every sound, like the whole world has fallen so silent, a pin dropping would deafen me. I listen for sirens, I stare at doors, and I don't move. At all. I'm like a statue, frozen in fear. (I'd probably be naked, by the way; I always had an urge to either be naked, or wear women's underwear, two things I've never once wanted to do when I've not been on drugs.) The only time I'd move would be to rack up a new line, and the longer the day went on, the longer it would take me to achieve that. Sometimes just bending down to the table could take over an hour, because the later it got, the more I believed I was going to be killed or a swat team would arrive. By the way, just to be clear about the wank I was having, I wouldn't necessarily have an erection, but I didn't let that stop me. I'd just keep doing it until I was finished, which would take at least 12 hours. I'd smoke between 30 and 40 cigarettes in this time. Taking one out of the box and lighting it could also take half an hour.
- 4 a.m. – Send pre-written text to John. I'd have less than a gram left by this point, and I'd wait desperately to hear from him, praying to myself that he was awake. 99 per cent of

the time, he was. I didn't like him being in the house if Patrick wasn't there because he had done a shit in my sink once and I never forgot that. So, I would've requested in the text that he put the drugs in our letter box and to text me when he'd done it. This was how I got into arrears with him, because I never paid for the second drop-off of the night.

- 5 a.m. – Drugs are dropped off. I go to pick them up. Putting clothes on and walking to the front door and back, about 15 feet away, can take up to 2 hours. I would be sweating profusely, and could soak through my clothes during this trip.

- 7 a.m. – Rack up a line if I'm capable of moving, which was rarely, because by this point it's like rigor mortis was setting in, and, weighing in at 6 stone, I was as close to a corpse as somebody breathing can get.

- 7.30 a.m. – Alarm. One hour till I need to be on set. I'd spend the hour getting ready, changing my clothes if I'd drenched them, and hopefully finish the wank. That was always like a reset for me, as soon as that had happened the paranoia would lift enough for me to get to the car, open the windows, and drive to work. And it would start again. I wouldn't sleep for anything between 36 and 72 hours at a time.

This is the most honest description I can give you without exaggeration, and I did this every day, for 6 months, at a cost of over £35,000.

And it came at a heavy cost in so many other ways.

At first I had stopped drinking alcohol with cocaine, preferring to sip on barley water during my days-long coke binges, like I'd just won the first set of the mixed doubles final at Wimbledon. But in those final months before entering rehab I'd started drinking heavily.

I was using alcohol to tamp down the effects of the cocaine. Which is like fixing a small hole in one knee of your jeans by setting fire to them.

This did nothing to help me sleep and just accelerated my physical deterioration. My heart was struggling to cope with the strains I was placing on it and the first physical symptoms of just how ill I was started to become obvious. I was sweating a lot. Not 'holiday in Spain' a lot or 'dose of the flu' a lot. 'Doing a 50km run through the Amazon jungle wearing a tweed suit' a lot. I looked like a lawn sprinkler with legs but I convinced myself, 'Well, it's getting towards summer, so that'll be why.'

As well as my health going downhill, my coping strategies had escalated. Drugs made doing the simplest of tasks take literally hours. You could watch *The Godfather* trilogy in the time it took me to go to the corner shop and back. I had so many checks, fears, paranoid thoughts, routines, sub-routines and contingency plans that I needed to rattle through in my head before I could face any task.

One morning, I was getting ready for work, which at this point took hours because I was going insane. I stood up to walk to the front door, which was only 30 feet from the sofa. This journey literally took several hours. The nearer I got, the more I sweated. Whole-body sweats, like my body was crying. I propped myself against the wall, using the radiator as a railing, and shouted at myself to calm down. I opened the door and eased myself down the stairs to the front yard.

I slid slowly down each step like a toddler, being punched in the ribs from the inside as I navigated every single stair, trying to get my breathing back under control. It felt like I was Ripley with an alien trying to force its way out of my chest.

Somehow, I still got to work. It was only years later that damage shown on an ECG scan confirmed that I'd had a heart attack. If you want to know how committed an addict is to drugs, I had a heart attack, pulled myself together and went to work to earn more money to buy more drugs.

'What doesn't kill you makes you stronger' can also be distorted into the addict's mindset. That heart attack hadn't killed me, so it wasn't a good enough reason to stop taking drugs. I finished the day's shooting, came home and carried on where I'd left off. In my head, days weren't divided by the clock or calendar. When a day at work ended, a new day of drug-taking started. The heart attack was yesterday, so it didn't count. This is the insanity you accommodate.

This is the place that rehab saved me from. This is the place I would return to within two weeks of getting out of rehab. Addicts don't reset, if we go back, we don't go back to a relaxed sip. We pick up where we left off.

Relapse

In many ways I left rehab in a *worse* state than when I arrived. OK, I was no longer days away from my body packing up on me and I now weighed more than a ten-year-old gymnast, but I'd learned a whole new set of ways to hide my addiction from others, thanks to speaking with the other patients. Like when a teenager goes to jail for shoplifting and comes out knowing how to rob banks and manufacture crack. I went in as someone doing lots of drugs but essentially very bad at hiding it. And came out with a whole new set of strategies.

I was the only person there who was doing their first stint in rehab. One guy there was on his sixth time. My first reaction to hearing this was to think, 'Well, this clearly isn't helping, is it?' I just assumed these repeat offenders weren't doing the rehab properly and were just fucking it up, like people who keep failing their driving test.

The way it worked was that, once you were booked in, you could choose from a range of addiction therapies available, like shopping from a catalogue (which, ironically, included a course on shopping addiction).

From what I could gather, it didn't seem to be massively tailored to you specifically, you just kind of tagged along with where they'd got to on a rolling plan for the period you were there.

One Thursday, I was sat in my room and a nurse knocked on my door and asked if I wanted to see the horse. I'd only been there a few days and I thought this must be some kind of test and surely the correct answer was 'no'.

As I was thinking this, a Shetland pony walked past behind him. It turned out that every other Thursday for three hours they'd have a Shetland pony walk around for the patients to say hello to.

'How are you feeling?'
'I want to die.'
(Brings a tiny horse into your room)
'How about now?'

To be fair, I defy anyone not to feel a bit better after seeing a tiny horse.

Despite all this, and the pretty fundamental objections I had to some of the concepts at the heart of their programme, once I'd got home that day, I felt that I had achieved something by completing my course, hence the champagne.

After a glass and a half, I had already tried to call my dealer's number but I realised I no longer had it and had no way of finding it again. The bottle of champagne soon disappeared and was followed by bottles of whatever else was in the house. A few days later, Patrick asked the reasonable question: 'So you spent a month at rehab and all you learned is that you're OK to drink?'

I wasn't OK to drink, though. I also needed drugs.

When you lose your dealer's phone number and do a month in rehab that most of your friends and family are aware of, it's not the easiest thing in the world to find out his number again. I called friends who were mutual customers and they not unreasonably refused to give it to me.

I knew one friend had John's number but I also knew he wouldn't give it to me if he thought it was for me. So I told him I had a friend called Keith who wanted some coke and gave him Keith's number. Keith's number was actually a burner phone I'd bought before contacting this friend. I had the chance to call Keith whatever I wanted – Zeus, Rumpelstiltskin, etc. – but decided to pick something inconspicuous.

Sure enough, Kev texted 'Keith' and I pretended to be Keith. A few weeks previously I had been in therapy, pretending to be an addict with a plan for the future, now I was pretending to be a man called Keith. It felt quite method because, like Keith, I really wanted some drugs.

I hadn't had so many acting gigs at the same time in my life. My friend gave 'Keith' John the Dealer's number and I kept the burner phone for ordering drugs. (To be clear, John the Dealer's real name wasn't John either.)

At this point my drug-taking changed dramatically. I now had a frame of reference of what 'help' looked like and it looked terrifying. Asking for help means you go from it being a solitary problem to everybody knowing. They all want to help you and you want them to fuck all the way out of examining your life. Help feels like a hindrance. My dealer knew I'd been to rehab and the first time he came round for a drop-off he asked, 'Are you sure you wanna do this?' When a coke dealer asks you that question, take it from me – it is a bad sign.

If anything, I was justifying my continuing habit to him. Not that he took a huge amount of persuasion. I explained that he had bills to pay, a mortgage to keep up and I would feel awful if I was the reason he couldn't do that because I'd stopped buying drugs from him.

Like most relapsing addicts I told myself if I was going to start taking again, I would at least try taking less. This lasted exactly one session and I was back to where I had left off. Everyone around me knew I had relapsed straight away, the signs were all there.

The Road to Rock Bottom
The first thing that I learnt when I got to rock bottom is that it's got a basement.

After an 'event' in the flat (more on this in the next chapter), it was strongly advised I move back with my family to see if this would change things. I'll let you guess if it did.

Amidst all this, I continued to work. The production company did everything they could and worked with my family to sort out a schedule of transport and chaperones to ferry me to and from work. To the outside world, I had a problem, but I had sought help and was now in a better place.

On top of the general toll on mental health a habit will take, I now also had guilt. Guilt that people had gone out of their way to help me and I had failed them and failed myself. I would delete John's number but it didn't work. I was a mess of alcohol and cocaine and antipsychotic medicine rehab had prescribed based on the lies I'd told them.

I even drew up a contract of promises and pledges that I signed and got all my family to sign:

Dear Family,
I promise that I will never drink again.
I will __not__ do drugs again and I will never lie to you all again.
I will do everything I can every single day to prove to you that
*   I've changed.*
I love you, and I am so desperately sorry.
Your boy,
Joe xx

I got drunk the night I signed it.

I was in no position to be trusted or to trust myself. I'd rejected everything I'd been told about dealing with my addiction. After two months of increasingly erratic behaviour, I decided it was the right time to go on a road trip.

A friend was in a show we both knew was so irredeemably shitty it wouldn't last more than a few performances. To avoid missing it, I drove a 140-mile journey that was a lot longer than I'd expected, because obviously I hadn't bothered to check how far away it was.

My friend had never been to rehab and knew nothing about addiction so when I got to her, I could tell her anything I wanted about what a recovering addict is allowed to do. She would believe me, because why wouldn't she? We were friends, after all.

The thing with addiction is that very few people who haven't had it really understand it. I would play on this for the next few years, constructing in my head the kind of spider's web of interconnecting lines you see on the noticeboard in a conspiracy-theorist's bedroom. Rather than photos of UFOs, newspaper headlines and blog posts, my mental noticeboard would have elaborate diagrams for everyone I ever met with how sober they knew (or thought) I was.

Every social interaction would involve consulting this. 'OK, that person knows I'm still drinking but they don't think I'm drinking a lot, so I can be (x) drunk with them. But this person thinks I'm sober so I have to keep them away from each other. That person knows nothing about my problems so I'll probably see if I can score some E off her', and so on.

This went on in my head all the time and, as you can imagine, it's exhausting. What you're doing is trying to make sure nobody finds out who you really are. On top of the exhaustion is the anxiety of thinking that one day somebody might stumble across this thick, dark web of addict lies. But the other thing about a web, it's still a connection. I can see that the energy I put into the lies were about finding a version of me where I could be with other people, so I could drown out the chance of me ever being left alone with myself. I was finding a version of myself that was allowed to be with other people – performing a version that they would accept. All to minimise that time when it was just me and my thoughts.

After the show, my friend and I went with the cast to the pub across the road from the theatre, and I did a trick I'd often use to drink without people noticing how much I was drinking. I'd order a load of Sambuca shots for the table, way more than there were people. A few people might take a shot and then I could drink most of the rest without anyone noticing.

I'd estimate I'd had half a bottle's worth in a very short time and I remember nothing from that point on. Again, I'm indebted to those who were there to fill in the details, including people with fear in their eyes who say they remember having met me in Malvern a decade ago.

At some point I announced I was going to the toilet, left the pub, and started the drive back. I managed about half an hour of the 140-mile journey before I mounted a roundabout, became airborne and landed in the centre of it. Nobody was hurt in the incident, thankfully.

Two guys in the car behind got me out of my car, called the police and called the last number in my phone as I was presumably too drunk to let them know who to call. The last number in my phone was my friend and they told her I was obviously drunk and had had a crash. When the police arrived and asked who had been driving, I apparently told them, 'Me. I shouldn't be here. I'm drunk.' Like in the chaperoned house when I was 19, one problem I didn't have was immediately taking the blame when it was mine to take.

I was arrested and put in the police van just as my friend arrived. At the station, I was breathalysed. Anything under 35 mg and at least I wouldn't be charged with drink-driving. I blew 103 mg. Ah. I was interviewed and I told them about my recent rehab stay. They asked if I was a danger to myself. I'd just flown a car into a roundabout so I thought that was a redundant question, but nevertheless answered yes, I was. This meant I was strip-searched and had all my clothes taken from me. In a life where humiliation and I aren't strangers, that was the most humiliating 12 hours I've lived through. I was given black clothes made of foam to wear in the cell, making me look like SpongeBob SquarePants if he was a depressed ninja, and was allowed to sleep off the drink.

The next day I was interviewed again and, on the way from cell to interview room, somebody recognised me. I didn't have my glasses on so I couldn't see who. This was my first worry, that the outside world might start to learn about what I'd done and what kind of person I was. Police said I'd be charged, which wasn't a huge shock, and I was released on bail.

My family solicitor advised that court cases tend to be dealt with on a first come, first served basis. I was to arrive very early at court, before press arrive looking for any interesting-looking cases (although there was still a risk they'd see the listings and recognise my name). My family drove me to the hearing and when they stopped en route to buy petrol, I managed to sneak into the shop, buy a bottle of vodka and drink it all on the back seat without them noticing. A car crash still wasn't enough to loosen the grip alcohol had on me.

We arrived at 6.30 a.m. and managed to get the first hearing. I had no experience of court and expected it to be a grand chamber of oak panelling and dramatic outbursts from the lawyers. Instead it was a drab, functional room where both the judge and the arresting officers (there to present evidence) treated the thing like another day at the office. Which for them, of course, it was, but it did help to relax me. Things were so relaxed that, halfway through the hearing, the judge remembered it was his son's birthday and temporarily halted proceedings to text him.

The judge banned me from driving for two years and my licence was taken off me for four (I was too scared to get my blood taken to prove I wasn't still drinking, because I was). Given what had happened, this seemed entirely reasonable.

Although the case wasn't reported on, it was the first time my addiction had bled into the real world and was no longer something that just happened to me on my own, in my room, inside my own head. That changed things for me psychologically. My family were still concerned for me, they still scheduled with the producers on travel and filming timetables. I was to get the train up and down the country as an alternative to driving or being driven. This was bad but not the end of the world; things weren't so bad that they couldn't be worked around.

Two weeks later I climbed over the railings of a bridge.

When I look back at that period of my life, I can now see that the drink and the drugs were manifestations of my BPD, what I would come to call Mick.

What I have learned is that there are a lot of interconnected fears that go along with my fear of abandonment: fear of being alone with myself without drink or drugs to take the edge off me; fear of facing up to how I've treated people when I came out the other side; fear of not being worthy of not being abandoned. Fear of disappointing the people I most need to be proud of me. I don't want to suggest that I am in any way out the other side of a fear of abandonment. Just ask my current girlfriend what happens when she brushes her teeth.

To be clear: I. Am. Still. A. Fucking. Mess.

As with all cliches there is a substantial grain of truth to the 'how can you love someone else unless you love yourself' bullshit. I've always felt that I have more love to give someone else because I don't have any love for me. But being alone with yourself shouldn't be the worst thing you can think of. I can say that, for me, getting to a place where I could be alone with myself without drink or drugs was the key. It wasn't the key to everything, but it was the key to a new room.

Right now, there are billions of people in all kinds and configurations of relationship, feeling trapped, feeling lonely, feeling guilty. Wishing they were with someone new, wishing they were with someone from their past. So many people feeling like they're not good enough. That they haven't earned the right not to be left alone.

This is, on one level, completely normal. The greatest joy we get is from other people, so why wouldn't we fear the opposite? But I think what I've realised is that it's the urgency that needs to change.

If someone leaves you, that might be shit for a bit. But you won't blink out of existence.

You do not always have to be the smoking car wreck, or the sinking ship (and you certainly don't need a tiny horse to feel happy). These are things. You are not a thing. You have the capacity to matter a great deal to someone new who you haven't even met yet. If you stay in the world, you give yourself that chance.

Chapter Four

Feelings of Suicide and Self-harm

Recurrent suicidal behaviour, gestures or threats, or self-mutilating behaviour

'You're fine. It's all in your head.'

I've heard that a lot.

It's often used to minimise the severity of mental illness.

Yes. It is literally all in my head.

That's the bloody problem. I don't know about you, but I live in my head. My experience of everything – love, sandwiches, music, limericks, dogs – they all come to me through my brain, which is in my head. So something only being in my head isn't comforting, it's terrifying.

Because if suicidal thoughts happened on my leg, I'd be able to see it, and fix it. Best-case scenario you take some antibiotics, it clears up. Worst case, if it got really bad, they'd amputate it. That would be terrible, but I'd live. I'd be here.

If you're somebody who is, or has been, suicidal, you can't see it, and don't know a way of fixing it.

There's no best-case scenario, and the only thing you feel you can amputate is yourself. Your head. Because that's how you feel. As worthless and broken as an infected limb with no prospect of ever healing. Physical pain IS mental pain. You feel any pain because your brain tells you that you're in pain. The only difference with mental pain is that it starts and ends there.

On top of all that is the guilt you carry for, what you see as, ruining the lives of the people around you that care about you.

Suicide is often thought of as a selfish thing to do.

But people don't kill themselves because they're not thinking about the people they love. They do it because they are.

You can't live with yourself, and you can't bear to watch everybody else have to live with you too.

You love them too much. You can see the hurt you cause, the pain you put them through, and you want to take that away. For you and everybody else.

The only way to show them how genuinely devastated and sorry you are for who you've been and the things you've done is to go away for ever. The ultimate sacrifice. To leave them in peace so they can rest, and not have to worry about you all the time.

You know they love you, and you're ashamed of the fact you've not been capable of returning that love, and that you've abused it, and them.

You genuinely believe that everybody close to you would be better off without you in their lives. Because you keep being like this and doing these things and you can't stop.

None of this is true. It feels real to you. It is your reality, but this is your illness. It is not you.

Kill yourself.

My brain will tell me 'kill yourself' is a more viable option than driving somewhere because my train's been cancelled. If you hear those two words enough times, deserted, without help, then, at some point, you're going to listen.

Even if you have asked for help in the past, sometimes it's not enough. Because when it's the world against those words, sometimes the world won't win.

There is underlying shame and fear within any moment of happiness. As if the thoughts are asleep, and I'm scared that it'll wake them up. That they might hear my happy and be like, 'LADS, he's feeling good, let's do this.'

Imagine that, being terrified and ashamed of feeling OK. It is exhausting.

If you're thinking about taking your own life, generally it's because you're feeling one, all or more of these things.

I hate myself. I can't live with who I am. I can't live with the things I've done. Everybody will be better off without me. The self-hatred that exists in somebody that's suicidal is all-encompassing. When you feel like a hollow shell, you fill up easily. That's something that can quickly get you to a point where you just need the noise and the pain to stop.

One result of me talking about suicide in the way I have is that it's added another reason not to do it. (In the six months after Robin Williams's suicide, suicides in the US went up substantially and the two things are widely accepted as being linked. I think people think that if you have a brain like Robin's and still can't cope, they have no chance. If Patch Adams can't find a reason to live, neither can I.) I've had enough messages from enough people to know that my not doing it is helping them not do it. People send messages every day and I try and read and reply to all of them.

I'm aware that I can't kill myself now because I know it could result in somebody else doing the same. This doesn't stop Mick suggesting it every day, of course, and when I tell him no he just busies himself in creating a picture of a swinging noose that literally stays in my brain all day, blocking all my everyday thoughts, while he says 'noose, noose, noose' over and over again, like the world's worst earworm. He never stops trying to find a way. In my more hopeful moments I realise that there are a finite number of things Mick can feel bad about. There are fewer new situations Mick can sink his teeth into as fresh meat to convince me to kill myself. Unreliable as they sometimes are, the things I've done thousands of times come with processes that can stop Mick from using them. Every time they work, he tries harder.

I'll give you an example: eating a melon. I like melon. I buy melon in bulk, in those plastic pots, so I always have melon in the fridge. If I run out of melon, Mick will start telling me to kill myself. He'll say . . .

Mick: Kill yourself.

Me: No.

Mick: But you've got no melon.

Me: I know that

Mick: Kill yourself.

Me: Still no.

Mick: You could have an orange.

In the end I'm stood there getting chilly with the fridge door open, going round and round in a circle, trying not to kill myself because I've not got fruit I want.

Mick is always upping the ante. All I am to Mick is hands. He can't kill me without them. I'm in a very powerful position here because I'm typing this sentence with the hands that he wants to use.

If I'm on my own, not telling people about him wanting me dead, he will always offer up 'kill yourself' as the answer to any problem before showing me the other options.

Melons are not the only fruit. But kill yourself is Mick's first response. The orange is not provided to me as an option until I've declined death.

If reading descriptions of incidents of self-harm and suicide is potentially going to be bad for you, you should turn to page 106. I wish I could do the same but unfortunately it's my fucking life.

I am 24 years old and I am standing on a bridge getting ready to jump.

Though I didn't know it at the time (and haven't told you yet), I had been on this road for a while. I had decided to cut my wrists shortly after getting out of rehab but, in truth, I didn't really commit to this decision, like I'd failed to commit to a lot of other decisions at that point. I'd used a steak knife but had missed my veins. I was still alive, just with sore wrists. I didn't tell anyone about it at the time.

Looking back, I realise that I had done this sort of thing before.

When I was 16, the day before I had been due to leave for stage school, I had a row with my girlfriend at the time. As she stormed off, I punched a sign for a nearby burger bar. (Please take it as a given that I know behaving like this isn't OK. I have thought a lot about what it must feel like to be on the other side of behaviour like this. Part of writing a book is that you tell your story and run the risk of pushing other people into the role of walk-ons in the miraculous story of you. But I think about everyone who's ever been on the other end of me being an arsehole every single day.) The sign was screwed to a solid lump of oak and I snapped my hand in half. I woke the next day, due to set off for a few weeks of performing magic, to find it had swollen up like a balloon. I decided the best thing to do was nothing. No hospital, don't tell anyone, don't take any painkillers.

Many years later, X-rays would reveal that I'd managed to push the knuckle of my little finger on my right hand halfway between where it should be and my wrist. A right mess, in other words.

This is one of the many times in my life that I have made self-destructive decisions in very slow motion. There is a tendency to think of self-destructive decisions as fast ones. But part of the way my self-destruction has always manifested relates to my physical wellbeing. I've always had an aspect of low self-image and a slow form of self-harm common to BPD. I treat my body terribly where food is concerned and I still don't eat in a sensible way. An opened bag of Gummi Bears is an empty bag of Gummi Bears. I had to be told what that little strip of sticky tape on bags of crisps was for. 'Inhale' is probably the best description of how I eat chocolate. But I also leave going to the doctors until the last possible moment. How many people do you know who've ended up hospitalised with athlete's foot? In the same way that we shouldn't only care about the extinction of animals that look cute on a T-shirt, we definitely shouldn't only pay attention to the kind of self-destructive behaviour that feels energetic and glamorous. Sometimes it involves extremely painful feet.

The Next Attempt

A few weeks later, I took an overdose of antipsychotic medicine and, this time, what I did would be enough to kill me – tablets, washed down with alcohol. But again, some part of me wasn't fully committed to the attempt and I called 999 almost immediately.

Looking back, it became clear I had been spiralling, in freefall for a while. On one occasion, Patrick came back to the flat and heard an odd noise, so started filming on his phone just in case it was something that would need evidencing. It was me, on all fours, repeatedly headbutting the coffee table in the living room. He asked what I was doing. I tried to stand, but fell face-first onto the table, so he put me in my bed. I lit a cigarette, then put it out on my arm. (This is that 'event' I mentioned earlier). It was this that had meant Patrick said I had to move back home with my family for my own safety. No matter how bad you get though, you can always 'be OK' for a few days in order to pretend everything is fine now, nothing to see here, please go away, I just have a phone call I have to make, no, it's none of your business. After a short stay with my family, I convinced them (and myself) that I was well enough to have a short stay in the old flat.

It was just long enough to take an awful lot of drugs and try another overdose of tablets. Again, I gave myself an escape route because I didn't want to die, I just wanted to stop feeling like I did. I called an ambulance, then left the security gate and front door to the flat open so there'd be no delay in the paramedics getting to me. Despite all this, I tried my best not to make it look like I'd intentionally made a suicide attempt I wanted rescuing from because in my head I thought they wouldn't take it seriously.

Paramedic 1: Estimated overdose of tablets taken, high alcohol levels, commencing a . . . oh, hang on.

Paramedic 2: What?

Paramedic 1: Bit easy to get into this flat, wasn't it? Almost like he wanted us to?

Paramedic 2: Now you mention it, yes. Fucking time-wasters. OK, let's go. We'll come back when he means business.

They did take it seriously, of course, and took me to the hospital where my stomach was pumped. It might not shock you to learn that stomach pumps aren't much fun. Horrendous, in fact. I vowed never to attempt suicide again. Not by overdose, certainly.

My stomach purged of tablets and booze, I decided I'd had enough hospital for one day. I walked out of the ward and got a cab home. The police were waiting for me when I got there as I was clearly a danger to myself. They took me back to the hospital, where I ducked out once more and got another cab home. This happened three times in total, like trying to herd a suicidal sheep into a hospital bed. I could now add feelings of guilt for wasting everyone's time to the guilt I already felt on a daily basis.

Patrick was called from the hospital and he contacted my family to let them know what had happened. I was released into his care and he took me back to his girlfriend's flat. At the time she was on very heavy painkillers for a back problem. I managed to find them next to her armchair and with great care, stealth and patience, stole a load of them. I took them all, ran out of the flat and decided a more effective suicide method would be to run in front of a lorry.

The door slammed as I ran out, alerting Patrick. He ran after me, dragged me out of the path of oncoming traffic and onto the pavement by the scruff of my neck. I have no memory of any of this happening and have to rely on the testimony of others. I was so out of my head at this point, the ability to process and make memories was like trying to use a broken umbrella to knit smoke.

Eventually, family arrived to take me back to Kent to live on a permanent basis.

I continued to work, splitting my life between living in Kent and filming up north. Hiding what was really going on. I created an elaborate scenario in which work was the thing keeping me going, which wasn't a lie, and that I was in recovery, which was a lie. This prompted a three-month period where every week I'd do a new worst thing I'd ever done.

But I didn't stop. It's a survival instinct even though what you're doing is killing you. Your brain tells you, 'Well, you're not dead yet so something must be all right with this; keep going, you don't have another option.'

I continued to drink and do drugs. To try and disguise the effects of this, I also managed to manipulate the psychiatrist I was seeing into giving me increasing dosages of antidepressants and antipsychotics, as well as changing the types of medication. I knew my family were very tolerant of the side-effects of medical drugs when you're getting used to them, so I knew I could blame my chaotic state on the prescriptions. Which is not to say I didn't also take the prescribed medication on top of the booze and coke. Of course I did.

At this point, of course, Mick didn't exist in a fully formed state; it was more a general internal dialogue saying, 'Why don't you have more drink and drugs?'

At this point the way to harm myself then became things like stabbing myself in the head with a fork and clawing at my face, which even a brain like mine couldn't fabricate a rational excuse for doing. It's clearly a very desperate thing to do and, as irrational as I was at that point, I think I still realised rational people don't stab themselves in the face with a fork.

Roll the Dice

The self-destruction wasn't always so immediate. On one occasion I went to a casino with about £600 in my pocket. I did what I always did in a casino which was to immediately abandon the people I'd arrived with so I could ruin my life in peace. I somehow managed, drunk as I was, to turn £600 into £2,000. I sought out the people I'd come with, told them of my windfall, then went back to the roulette table and lost it all.

I put half of it on red. I lost. I put the other half on black, thinking I could at least get back to where I'd been fifteen seconds ago. I lost again. I couldn't face telling my friends what I'd done, so my habitual lying, lack of coherent thought and desire for self-harm came up with a plan.

I went into the toilets and comprehensively beat myself up. Not emotionally, I physically beat myself up, throwing myself around the room, self-assault. I broke a tap, I head-butted the sink, I threw myself into doors. When I decided I'd had enough, I left and found my friends. My injuries were immediately visible and they asked what had happened. Telling them wasn't an option so I said I'd been jumped for my winnings and we had to leave immediately.

As we left, I concocted an inside job involving the bouncers following me to the toilet to get the casino's money back, with one bouncer minding the door while the other roughed me up. I didn't realise that one very sensible friend I was with had gone back to the casino to tell the manager what I told her had happened. She came back with the manager and, balls-deep as I was in the lie, I couldn't back out so I told the same story to him.

'Fortunately, we have CCTV in the toilets,' he said. 'Not the cubicles, but the sink area where you said it happened. Let's go back and we can review the footage.' He seemed very sincere but there's also the chance he knew I was full of shit and was calling my bluff. Adding another boulder onto the mountain of bullshit I'd built, I feigned a panic attack, telling my friends that the manager was in league with the bouncers and was just trying to lure me back to the casino so they could beat me up again. I convinced my friends to take me back to my hotel instead.

The whole incident was never mentioned again.

I think any mental health problem, if you ignore it for long enough, will become a physical problem. It could be a week, it could be years, and this was what was happening to me.

Climbing over the rail of the bridge came from a feeling of utter exhaustion. Exhaustion with other people's hopes for me to be sorted as well as the exhaustion that comes from knowing I couldn't change what I was doing, I couldn't deal with having to see that face from my family one more time – that face of total disappointment.

With some people who fuck up all the time, they take the defensive position of telling you that this is who they are, so if you don't want to be with somebody who fucks up all the time, find somebody else to be around. But every single time it happened with me, I was genuinely sorry. There wasn't an ounce of me that didn't regret what I'd done. Which made it worse, especially after rehab, when things happened again. But there wasn't a day, even with a head full of drugs, where I didn't know the difference between right and wrong.

It was a total feedback loop. The best way to make sure you don't want to spend time with your own thoughts is to do things you feel objectively ashamed of. To lie to people you love. To borrow money and spend it on the one thing you've told them you won't spend it on. To do things that hurt you and them, again and again. Rationality wasn't connected to emotion at that point. I was genuinely sorry, but the next day it would happen again and that just made it even harder to continue to deal with. The disconnect between knowing this thing is harming you and those around you and knowing you're going to do it anyway. Those were the moments that got harder to live with – when my family knew it had happened again. You lose any memory of the good times as they're replaced with new memories of addiction and failure. It was relentless and I knew I was the cause of it, or at least I thought so at the time. I could feel people in my life checking out at very different stages of my deterioration.

At some point, my dad managed to get hold of Chip, who ran a residential rehab programme for people with serious drug habits. Dad obviously wanted to help because it was clear I was dying. But the only way Chip could possibly help was if I phoned him myself. His advice to Dad was to take a step back until I could help myself by asking for help.

One reason Dad didn't understand what was happening was that I would pretend things were fine when I was back home. I'd go up for work, fuck things up there, come home, they'd find out, then I'd start that cycle all over again. Chip told Dad that anybody can be OK for a day. Most can for two. At a push you can manage three. Nobody can do four if they're ill.

He gave my dad his details, which Dad passed on to me. It would be a while before I used them.

Jumping off the bridge wasn't to stop how I was feeling. Not the main thing anyway – it was more of an added bonus to the decision to know I wouldn't have to be me any more. It was actually a gift to everybody else, I thought. My family never had to have their faces crumple in disappointment and sadness at my latest fuck-up. I just couldn't look at them hurting that way any more, so this was my gift to them – stopping that from ever happening again. Stopping me from destroying their lives.

On the day in question, I'd been away for a long weekend for a friend's family birthday. On the way back home I went to see a musical in London that a friend was doing. All I'd ever wanted was to be on stage and I loved musicals.

After the musical I went with some of them to a casino (because, you know, that always ends well). I never book a hotel in advance when I go anywhere because that involves a level of forward planning that is beyond me, so I had my bags with me when we went there. I started drinking and immediately lost my sense of humour. This was a common feature back then and one that always scared me the most. Confident-appearing and affable Joe was my selling point as a person (even if I didn't feel that way inside) so to know it disappeared the second I had a drink or did a line was really frightening.

I left my friends and played poker for so many hours I lost track of time, drinking heavily. I kept winning. £300 became £1,500 and I didn't want any of it. But I was numb and tired. I just didn't care about anything. Not at a deep level. On a surface level I cared about my family, about not upsetting people, about basic social manners, but not in my bones.

I can see now that my behaviour up to the night in that casino was a succession of ways to hurt myself in order to feel something. Because the giant diffuse pain of being someone you despise, who is hurting everyone trying to take care of them, again and again and again, is too big. It has no edges, nothing to get a hold of. But the specific pain of hurting yourself somewhere with precision, that you can get your head around; that feels, from a certain angle, like control. Like breaking a big task into smaller more manageable tasks. That's just pain admin.

Here, in a situation in which I felt like even though I was trying to hurt myself but I kept winning, I just couldn't take it.

There was no lightbulb moment. There were no tears. I wasn't crying when I left the poker table. The only reason I left at that point was that I knew I was due to go back home to my family. There was no plan at that point. At about 3 a.m. I just got up and left. I had no idea where I was going and no direction in mind. I got to a bridge and threw the money in the water as a way to punish myself. I knew I didn't want to do the next day again and didn't want to do the everyday things I had to do ever again.

I didn't want to be me any more. I had no tools to improve my life. All I had was the last three months of hard evidence that all the help in the world wasn't enough. I was hopeless. Looking back, I'm more surprised that I didn't actually jump off that bridge. Given where my brain was at that point, all the odds were that I would do it. But somehow I didn't.

I wish I could tell you that in those darkest moments in your life and you turn things around, when you decide not to end it all, that you hear a heavenly choir singing, a golden light appears over your head and Morgan Freeman whispers wise advice in your ear. But life isn't like that. I just didn't throw myself to my death.

Which isn't to say, if future Joe had appeared that night and told me that I would think about killing myself constantly for the next decade and that this night on the bridge wouldn't even be the worst I'd feel, I might not have made a different decision. But I chose not to die then and as a result I'm not dead and there will be a future Joe and every day I don't do it, there'll will be a different future Joe and I think that's a good thing. I have to re-convince myself of that every day, but that doesn't change the fact that between being dead and not being dead, not being dead is a good thing.

On that particular occasion, another carrot on a stick enticing me away from the edge – and one I can definitely tell you is a bad idea – was the prospect of doing more drugs. So I climbed back over the railing and I called John and bought more drugs. He drove me back to Kent as I did them in the car, which was a sign of the low point I'd reached. In the face of everything I'd always been really fastidious about laying out my drugs somewhere private. John parked at the bottom of the drive so I could hide from my family and I never saw him again because I never did drugs again. At the time it felt the same as most other nights over the last ten years, except for my time on the bridge.

As with my decision on the bridge, there was no Hollywood moment that meant I never did drugs again. I'm sure some people have them but it never happened for me. In fact that's not entirely true; I did have big, dramatic days where I decided NEVER AGAIN but I know that every single time that happened, the next day would bring OH, GO ON THEN, AGAIN.

My mum stopped drinking for ever one day because she had a bit of a rough hangover. Other family members have quit drinking without any dramatic inciting moment. I think it's important that people know that today *could* be the day you stop doing that thing that's harming you. It doesn't need to be January 1st or on top of a mountain or with you shouting into the teeth of a thunderstorm. It could just be a Tuesday afternoon on your sofa. You don't know it's a significant day until one day looking back you realise it was.

Thinking it needs to be something dramatic to make you quit can just put pressure on you to make it a significant moment. I've seen friends jostling people into quitting and they're not in the right place for that to happen and it's a really bad idea. When you get clean it can make you evangelical and that can backfire really badly if your target isn't in the right place in their life.

This particular night I crawled into the garden and climbed up a tree to take the last of the drugs. However, I'd forgotten I'd left bags on the doorstep, so when everyone woke up, they knew I'd come home but wasn't in my room. For three hours, I listened to them calling for me, worrying I had killed myself and talking about me. Then the neighbours told them I was up the tree.

The Call

The next day, I phoned Chip. I felt I was ready to at least try and see if I could not do this any more. I was sitting with my mum at the time in the back garden and I knew I needed to change. What I wanted was to go to him immediately so he could save my life. A typical addict's selfishness that the world needed to change for them. But this new place wasn't like Fancy Rehab and you couldn't just phone and tell them you'd be there the next day. As a charity dealing with NHS referrals and people leaving prison, availability was limited.

Chip was glad I'd gotten in touch and said he would see me in a week's time. Both I and my mum panicked. I think

I collapsed on the floor and stayed there for a while. I didn't need help in a week, I thought, I needed it now.

While bed availability may have been one reason for the week's wait, the main reason was to see if you were ready for the help being offered. If you couldn't wait a week and still want to go, you probably weren't ready. Fortunately my current psychiatrist managed to find a hospital ward where I could be safe until then. Not a secure ward; I was free to leave whenever I wanted, and that was important. Because anyone can avoid drugs and alcohol if there's a lock on the door stopping you getting to them. That's not recovery, that's escapology.

After my week on the ward, I went to Focus, which I can confidently say saved my life. Eventually.

I realise for anyone looking for answers to the meaning of life, the key to not killing yourself being 'don't kill yourself' is likely to feel somewhat unsatisfying. But that's what has done it for me. If I have one wish for this book, it would be that it makes one person one small bit more likely to tell someone they want to kill themselves. That it makes one person one bit more likely to check in on someone in a bad place.

People don't talk about it because people don't talk about it. The only way it's usually referenced in the media is in the high drama Hollywood, I-can't-go-on manner. But it's not always like that. Suicidal thoughts are often, like mine, a mundane daily grind of thinking about causing your own death. The more matter-of-factly I talk about it in public, the more I hope other people feel like they can do the same.

If 'I've been thinking about killing myself' could be talked about in the same tone as 'I'm thinking about getting a tattoo', or 'I'm thinking about learning Portuguese', stripped of its melodrama while being taken deadly seriously, more people would feel like they could say it.

People feel such a great weight to solve a situation, that they don't know what to say. That anything they say might make things worse. I promise you won't. Sit there. Tell them you don't want them gone from the universe. That's it. There will be other things that need to happen when someone is in that place. There will be professionals, there will be advice.

But in that first instance, it will be enough. In *many* instances it will be enough. One person being with another person. Making them realise that the overwhelming feeling that everything would be better without them in the world is wrong.

You might be sat there on your own without another person. But I'm here (I know I'm not *there* with you). Wherever you are, I know that the hardest thing you do every day is breathe. I also know that everybody who's ever cared about me would rather I told them I was thinking about killing myself than try to do it. The same is true for you.

Sometimes, when I'm thinking about killing myself, the only thing I need is somebody to tell me not to.

So, please don't kill yourself.

*

'All children, except one, grow up.' That's the first line of *Peter Pan*, my favourite book.

Unfortunately of course it isn't true.

Not all children grow up. (And clapping doesn't bring someone back when they're dead, though I am aware of the irony of being a suicidal performer in this context. Every little helps.)

Peter is scared to grow up and I get it. Growing up is scary. It involves pain and lots of things that are much less fun than flying and fighting pirates. Like mortgage applications and cancer and being responsible for the boiler and heartbreak and being left and being lied to and being hurt and bereavement and financial advisers and job interviews and car accidents and buying toilet paper and miscarriages and commuting and sorting out the gutters and marriage and childbirth and becoming an orphan and a million things that we cannot predict and we cannot control. Life is a mixture of joy and terror and surprise and endless overwhelming feelings.

Feelings aren't a choice. We don't choose how we feel. The only choice we have is whether or not to tell someone about it.

But we all deserve the chance to grow up. That is an awfully big adventure.

Chapter Five

Extreme Emotional Swings

Affective instability due to a marked reactivity of mood

Let me take you through a day in the life of extreme emotional swings, based on what I did yesterday:

- 9 a.m.: Wake up to the sound of workmen drilling the road outside and loathe all workmen, drills and roads with a passionate intensity. Hope that they all get drilled to death with their own drills, then buried under the road they just dug up.
- 9.02 a.m.: Put on socks still warm from the radiator. Feel an intense sense of comfort and contentment of the kind usually experienced by gurus who have meditated on top of a mountain for thirty years and can breathe through their belly button. I have never known such bliss.
- 9.03 a.m.: Actually, my feet are a bit hot now. Who the fuck invented socks and why weren't they stoned to death as soon as they started knitting the first pair? Tear the socks off my feet and throw them across the room, vowing never to wear socks again.
- 9.05 a.m.: Walk into the bathroom and my feet are a bit cold on the tiles. Gripped with an overwhelming sense of regret at taking off my socks and beat myself up because

of my hasty sock decisions, which are just an emblem of all the bad decisions I've made in my life.

I haven't even brushed my teeth yet (revulsion that I don't floss as often as I should, etc.) and I have a whole day of this to come. I want you to imagine a six-year-old child moving through their day. A friend not wanting to play with them is the end of the world. Their teacher telling them off a disaster. The wrong food at lunch something to be worried about at bedtime. A succession of intensely felt feelings that threaten to overwhelm them, that aren't subject to logic or experience, that can't be reasoned with. Each one the worst thing ever. A tiny boat tossed on the storm of their emotions.

That's me. That's my day every day.

This, along with my already mentioned inability to learn from previous scenarios about likely future outcomes for myself, means I'm incapable of perceiving the actual threat level of a problem. I react to a possible dirty look on a bus with the same emotional response as if a loved one told me they hate me. Unfortunately, I don't get it the other way around. No crying with joy looking at a fucking plastic bag floating in the breeze for me.

The people in my life have had to get used to me crying, a lot.

How Are You?

What I have learned is that 99 per cent of people don't actually mean the question 'How are you?' literally. Because when you answer honestly it really weirds them out. When people ask me, on a good day I answer that 'I'm still here.' On a bad day, it's 'Not dead yet.' Honest, but not freaking them out. 'How are you?' is probably the second most common question that comes out of my mouth, too. The first is, 'Have I upset you?' It turns out I never have. My brain just has an exhausting habit of painting angry faces onto people that aren't actually angry at me.

It's not just me opening every chat with 'How are you?' It's all of us. But we're not asking because we care, we're asking because we're British. The problem with using 'How are you?' as a form of manners, is that we never know what to do with the answer. If it's anything other than 'Good, you?', we're knackered.

But what happens if we ask somebody that's not OK how they are, and they actually tell us? Well I am the person behind the book that is in front of you, and I am not OK. But I will be. I don't know when, but I will.

I know because out of my 34 years here, I've been not OK more than I've been OK. I know I've always come out the other side because I've always woken up, even on the days that I didn't want to. And even if my problems haven't gone away or I've got more than I had the day before, the only time I won't be able to fix something is if I'm not here.

And I am here.

So there's hope.

My threshold for things that make me feel upset is very low. I will buy a sausage roll and, later that day, Mick will tell me the woman I bought it from hates my guts. With no supporting evidence. This would be annoying but manage-able. But Mick keeps saying it. And keeps saying it. So much so that all other thoughts get blocked out. I can't achieve anything else while those thoughts go on and it shoves rational thought out of the frame. And with my lack of emotional control, such a thought would make me want to start sobbing rather than feel mild disappointment.

But I can buy my sausage roll, give a sheepish smile and ask the woman behind the counter, 'This will sound really weird, but are you angry with me?' and when she invariably doesn't know what I'm talking about, I can tell Mick to get back to his room. It does make him angrier, it does make him work for a few days on stuff that's even worse, but it does tell him that he's failed. For today, at least.

The thing is that because I know at any moment things will switch, I can't even really enjoy the happy bits. I spend a lot of time being honest to those close to me about how unhappy I am. So that's their consistent message. If I then tell them I'm feeling happy, it makes me worry they won't believe me when I'm unhappy once more. It makes me wonder if they'll think I'm lying about being unhappy. And it's even worse if someone tells me something I have said or done has made them happy. At that point my default thought is how shit it's going to feel for both of us when I'm at my very worst again.

Also, these days, Mick is a clever little shit about this. He sees me doing well and decides to stay quieter for longer. If he's always in my ear, it's background noise and I can tune him out. For him it's a very intellectual game, like chess with a computer. He's looking at all the moves and it's possible to beat him, but it's really hard. He'll wait for the optimum time to make his move.

I know some people mask – act the outward show of emotions they've learned are normal so people know they are actually feeling them – but I can't do that. Because I find it difficult to regulate my emotions through the day as it is, throwing in a quick performative sob into the mix would just confuse the life out of me. My other least favourite phrase, one which I heard every other day throughout lockdown, is 'I mean, what's happening to me isn't that bad though, some people have it so much worse'. Saying you shouldn't be sad because people have it worse is like saying you shouldn't be happy because somebody has it better.

If you're feeling something, feel it. Don't apologize for it. Your feelings aren't a mistake, and neither are you.

And this is how things are at the best of times. Now imagine how big the swings were when I was learning to live without drugs and doing therapy in rehab.

I am 27 years old and am stood very still in a kitchen while a very large scary-looking man laughs at me because I am holding a raw chicken. I will never know what he finds so funny about this particular chicken. I am in the kitchen with Colin as part of the rehab programme I have just entered, who I've been asked to buddy up with for a fortnight.

He was six foot three, bald, built like a shed, had a chain-smoker's cockney growl and was straight out of prison. Behind his terrifying exterior, he had a gentle demeanour and seemed a sweet person. But, as we walked from the centre back to the accommodation, I learned a valuable lesson about not asking questions you don't want the answer to. I was still learning how to talk to people without the scaffolding of drugs or playing a character and was told to be honest all the time. In conversation I asked what he'd been in prison for and he told me rape.

I had no idea what to do with that information; all I knew was I had to spend the next fortnight almost entirely in his company. He went on to say he'd been a career criminal, mostly robbery, since he was ten.

So one day, I'm alone in the flat with him and I can hear him in the kitchen laughing to himself, which is not a sound you want to hear from a bloke you're terrified of. I conquered my fear and went to see what he was laughing at which, it turned out, was a raw oven-ready chicken he was cradling like it was a baby.

He asked if I'd seen this chicken, which I had. He then asked me to take his picture holding the chicken, which I did because, as I may have mentioned, I was terrified of him. He then asked me if I wanted my picture taken with the chicken – which I *absolutely did not* – but again, terrified, I agreed.

I still have the photos on my phone. The first is of a shaven-headed man whose frame fills the doorway holding a raw pre-packed chicken. He is absolutely fucking delighted with the chicken. The second is of me, who appears to be half a mile away in comparison, such is the size difference, with the same chicken and the very obvious expression of a man who would rather be anywhere else on the planet. If you wanted to find a pictorial representation of an extreme emotional swing, just flick back and forth between Colin holding the chicken and me.

Focus

The place they got me into, where I would eventually meet Colin, was called Focus. Compared to Fancy Rehab, it was rough. It was a very different place and, clearly, I thought this would be a good thing as I had come to feel the previous rehab hadn't helped me at all. I'd seen a documentary about it so I was aware of it as potentially a good place to be. It didn't feel clinical, which I liked, as Fancy Rehab had felt like *One Flew over the Cuckoo's Nest,* if they'd put some carpet down.

You'd walk through reception and there were three photos on the wall. Boy George, Russell Brand and Davina McCall. All previous graduates of Focus and now patrons of the charity. I used to talk to Davina, or rather her photo, all the time. When I opened the door in the morning I'd nod hello and on my way back to the accommodation I'd stop to tell her how I did that day. I'd never met her and I didn't know her but it felt nice to update her on my progress. There were times where it helped keep me going. Because I didn't want to let Davina down. (More recently, I was able to contact Davina and tell her how much she'd helped me. As I mentioned, we'd never met but she seemed like an achievable example of somebody who had their act together. When I had bad days where I worried I'd drink again, I'd think, 'No, don't. Davina wouldn't do it.')

There's no cotton wool in this rehab. Just a house with a load of meeting rooms and a garden with what was essentially a shed in it. And the shed is where the therapy sessions happened, eleven hours a day, six days a week. You got the day off on Sunday but were expected to use your day off to go to an AA or an NA meeting.

I'd initially agreed to be there for three weeks as I had a panto job I'd committed to. Work had always been a central thing for me so, in my head, playing Buttons was more important than working on not dying. Focus don't ordinarily do bespoke programmes – you're there for three months because that's how long it takes – but they had agreed to an initial three weeks for me.

The original plan was to do three weeks of Focus, then panto, then back to work. But it became clear very quickly that I wanted and needed to do the full course. Work had told me that they could only spare me for the three weeks plus panto and I wasn't allowed any further time off. So when I called to say I would actually be away for months, I was doing it in the belief I would essentially be handing in my notice. This was a scary prospect and I'm still proud of myself that I made the decision I did knowing this could happen.

I called the producer and told him my revised schedule, expecting the worst. Instead they told me to take as much time as I needed to get better and just keep in touch with them, which was an incredibly generous thing for them to do.

For the first couple of weeks I was quite casual about being there. It seemed OK and seemed manageable. I really committed to all the written work and exercises but I was also aware that I had the ability to do all the outward stuff you have to do in rehab while still holding a lot of stuff back. How to make it convincing enough to fool the therapist. I knew deep down that this was what I was actually doing.

Fortunately there was a therapist there who was 100 per cent smarter than I'll ever be and she saw through my bullshit in a heartbeat. When they agreed to let me go do panto, she and the other therapists laid down very clear conditions: I was to be breathalysed and drug-tested on my return. I was accompanied on the journeys there and back – the panto was too far away for me to stay at Focus, hence the three-week break.

None of these conditions stopped me from drinking the moment I got to the shared house I was staying in for the panto run. My addict's brain patted me on the back for doing a bad thing but not a worse thing – one guy in the house smoked weed and I didn't join in. Pat on the back for drunk Joe, he stayed off the drugs while he was pissed. It's all part of the hierarchy of addictions in rehab. On the one hand, addicts can look up or down on the substances the other people were addicted to depending on what they were. But on the other hand, there's a snobbery about how low you got at your worst – a race to the bottom of how badly you behaved. But ultimately, with addiction, you'll eventually get to the point where you'll have whatever's going. A heroin addict won't turn their nose up at a six pack of strong lager if that's what's on offer.

My level of drinking started at exactly the point where I'd left off. The level of work I did wasn't affected, or at least was only as affected as it had been for the last few years when I was drinking and using drugs. One odd thing about rehab is that people you only know from that context can only view you in that context. A therapist from Focus came up to see me in panto and told me he cried because

'Performing Joe' – competent, confident, talented – wasn't a person he'd met before. Because I was so ill with addiction it was hard for him to see me in any other light.

I was really scared because, for everything I'd filmed in the last five years, I hadn't slept the night before because I'd been up all night on drugs. It was a standard way of working as an adult and I used it as an excuse to carry on drinking and taking drugs because I told myself this was the way I worked. I had convinced myself it was like an athlete's lucky pants, or someone taking a toy into an exam hall.

When I finally get clean, I will look back at those days of performing magic as a kid, because I knew that was something I was really good at and it was something I did sober. It showed I had the ability to be good at things without the drugs and the drink.

Obviously, I knew I would be breathalysed when I returned from panto, so I made sure I stopped drinking long enough beforehand that I would blow a clean reading. You will never find a happier person in creation than an alcoholic who hasn't drunk doing a breathalyser test. They will <u>demand</u> that you stuff that tube in their mouth. They will knock on doors and gather people round to witness the clean reading they're about to give. Like a shoplifter with empty pockets getting searched by police. I was very proud of my clean reading despite knowing it only happened because I was hiding my drinking in the kind of way only an alcoholic knows how to.

It was a shit thing to do and it was a shit lie to maintain, both to my family and the people at Focus who were just trying to help me. But I feel enough time has passed where I can let go of what I did. If I had told my family when it happened, it would have ended any hope they might have clung on to that I would ever get clean and, obviously, I would have been kicked out of Focus. I'd have deserved it, I am aware of that, but this is what happened. I just hate that when I was an addict I was letting my family down all the time and I haven't had that feeling for a while and I have to tell them that, actually, there's one more thing to add to the list.

I returned to Focus with an honest intention of getting the most out of it, despite knowing it was based on a falsehood. It was time to start the therapy sessions once more.

The sessions took the form of group therapy, which is essentially a three-month facilitated argument in a room with a load of people at various stages of sobriety.

Have you ever had really bad pins and needles? When the blood has been cut off from your arm and leg and then comes rushing back in and it really fucking hurts? That's what it felt like going through the process of therapy in rehab after feeling so numb. I was feeling things without the drugs and booze being in the way for the first time in years.

The best thing about being in rehab is that you get your feelings back, and the worst thing about it is you get your feelings back.

I was confronting things that I had ignored or never known what I was feeling before, at the same time as dealing with the extremity of group therapy. Any one of these things would have been enough on their own. All together, it was overwhelming.

Group therapy takes a long time to get used to. A big element of the therapy is getting you to recognise yourself and elements of your addiction in other people. The therapist, who acts as a referee, will introduce a topic that gets discussed by everyone in the group and how it relates to their own experiences. (I had been in therapy since the age of 21. But that involved avoiding talking about the things I should have been talking about with a nice man called Alan who had jet-black hair in a bowl cut that looked like it was drawn on his head with a Sharpie pen.)

It's an atmosphere that's the polar opposite of how you're taught to behave as a functioning adult. Most people's default behaviour in a new environment is to try and be polite, not be overly revealing about your own life.

Group therapy is the complete opposite. You have to be totally honest about everything. If you decide in these sessions to stop being honest, or if somebody else just decides that you're not being honest, they can and will call you up on it. Because this is a large part of your waking life for such a long time, you very quickly stop noticing how odd a way to behave this is in real life. You were turning up every day to tear them a new arsehole because they weren't entirely frank about something they may have done five years ago.

Lie in the Sky

As a liar, I found the whole process both incredibly helpful and incredibly frustrating. Not least because when you're a liar you assume everyone is lying all the time because that's how you process the world. Also because, as an actor, it was the easiest accusation for others to throw at me. I'd be told I wasn't being genuine and that, as an actor, I was trying to get one across the group. But you can't really lie in that room, at least not for very long. One reason is that you talk less about events (which was the usual subject of most of my dishonesty) and more about emotions and thoughts (that I'd not really talked about, and which was probably part of the problem). Either way, lying is a lot harder when you have fifteen other fact-checkers in the room.

That said, I did lie about some things in that room, my drinking during panto being the most obvious one, and I still regret having done that. I overcompensated this massive lie by going back to group session and turning my arsehole dial up to eleven. I slated everyone for the dishonesty I perceived in others and challenged them constantly. The therapist loved this, as I'd been overly polite previously and they viewed my new, assertive manner as taking a more active part in sessions when all I was really doing was projecting my own behaviour onto others as a diversion. I came back with something to hide and it made me a complete arsehole.

The living arrangements kept you more honest, too. The treatment centre itself was a building with no living quarters in it. The charity had five properties in about a mile's radius around this building. Each property had several bedrooms that you'd stay in during the three months of your treatment. If you were exhibiting any behaviours in your accommodation that were potential red flags (such as spending too much time alone, a favourite of mine), a flatmate would rat you out in the next session. Because honesty included calling out other people's behaviour when you saw it.

These living arrangements served another purpose. To walk to and from the treatment centre you had to walk past pubs and drug dealers. The drug dealers were there because Focus was there. They knew they had a captive audience of potentially relapsing addicts. The thinking behind this was that, for the therapy to work, it had to work in the real world. There's no point staying clean for three months in an environment where there's no other option. It's like being stranded on a desert island and taking a vow of chastity. Piece of piss on an island, mate. To be honest about your desire to get better, you had to walk past these temptations and not give in to them. And when you weren't honest, it was the job of the therapists and other patients to criticise you for it.

It wasn't just about criticism. You would also give praise to people who had done something well, either in their current progression or in how honest they'd been about things they'd done in the past. One shoplifter proudly announced he'd not stolen anything for 24 hours and got a round of applause, which is not a thing you'd be praised for in any other environment. But it was about acknowledging how much the small things fed into the big things.

By having people at different stages in their rehab all in the same therapy sessions, you had positive reinforcement each day that it could work. There was one guy in his sixties, basically up for his Lifetime Achievement Award in alcoholism, and I watched the therapy work for him and watched him graduate determined to stay clean in a way I entirely believe he managed. It genuinely made me think that if it could work for him, it could work for a relative newbie like me.

Then there were times that somebody would eventually open up about something horrific in their past and all of the pieces of their behaviour up to that point would fall into place.

One specific guy could be, bluntly, a bit of a twat. Nice guy, bit of a twat. His contributions in therapy were usually pretty glib until he told a story about how he was domestically violent towards the mother of his kids. She was pregnant when he beat her so badly, she was hospitalised. In another wing of the same hospital was his mum, who was seriously ill and had been taken to hospital the same night.

Due to the history of violence, there was a social worker and police officer waiting to take his kid away as soon as it was born. Because he was drunk and high, he didn't consider that would happen. So in the space of one evening he dashed to one side of the hospital too late to see his mum before she died, then dashed back to the other too late to see his latest kid before it was taken into care.

Alongside the structured verbal abuse, there was also a lot of written work. So just imagine you're dealing with all of the lies you've built up about yourself smashed apart. Often, you've had someone shouting at you for being dishonest. And then you've got to do admin. You were given various written tasks and the dreaded feedback sheets. Every single week with the feedback sheets.

At any point in group therapy you can have between six and fifteen people in a session at one time. You would be given a feedback sheet to fill in about every person in that session. If this sounds like an awful thing to have to go through, remember that filling in fifteen feedback sheets about other people means that fifteen feedback sheets about you were on their way.

They would ask whether you thought somebody was doing well and why you thought so. Did you think they were going to fuck up their lives again? Why? What three things about this person do you like? Do you dislike? It's essentially a character assassination formatted like a customer satisfaction form and it takes ages to complete because you've got hours and hours of therapy to draw from for your answers.

And then you had to read them out in front of each other.

Once everyone has finished furiously scribbling away, occasionally looking up to remind themselves of the person they're writing about, they get given all the feedback sheets others have written about them. A big stack of opinions on why you're a terrible person written by people you've just said is a terrible person on the form you filled in about them. A load of opinions you didn't want from people whose opinions you don't necessarily respect. A paper version of Twitter.

Can you begin to imagine the arguments that would prompt? It was about breaking down the barriers they – and I – all had that stopped us getting to the truth. These weren't just the defensive barriers we'd built up about our own addiction, it was the general social and conversational barriers we all have as adults.

I'm not going to ever suggest that everyone should go through the full process, but most of us put zero thought into thinking about what makes us feel something and why. We treat our emotions a bit like weather – here comes a storm, ooh a lovely sunny day, what a nice surprise. A tiny amount of thinking about emotions, how they arise, what patterns there are in their creation feels incredibly empowering. When I use something I learnt now to try and head off a negative emotional situation, I can imagine how the person who pioneered weather forecasting felt the first time they opened their umbrella.

It's a constant battle and I wish I didn't have to do it, but I do look back on how I've done in a day, to take responsibility for my own problem. It isn't my fault that I have Mick but I have to do whatever I have to do to control it. I don't have a choice; I either do it or I die.

If the crossfire of frank opinions and outright insults from other patients weren't enough, the therapists would chip in during sessions as well, like a boxing referee who throws in the occasional right hook when he thinks things have gone a bit quiet.

Once a week there would be art therapy and, my god, I hated art therapy. I knew I was going to die because I was a drug addict and I didn't feel collages were the answer. Over 90 minutes I would be encouraged to draw or paint or create something. Some would try their best because they liked it, some were rubbish but would still have a go and some (me) would do it under protest, acting the arsehole the whole time because they hated it.

During the session, the therapist would walk around, commenting on what people were doing, like Ainsley Harriott on *Ready Steady Cook* but, instead of their take on a bolognese, it was a smackhead doing a drawing of a clown. I'm sure it helped some people, but I've yet to meet an ex-addict who says the thing that keeps them away from the bottle is doing a watercolour every other Tuesday.

As much as I hated art therapy I still have all the things I made in those sessions. I've resisted the urge to burn them, even now. Even though I hated the sessions, it was about showing up. Part of rehab is learning that you have to do things you don't want, when you're meant to do them, and not just quit because it's a pain in the arse.

That's what everyday life is once you're sober – a series of turning up, even when you don't want to. I might fuck up once I'm here, I might want to leave as soon as I arrive, but you asked me to be here at 9 a.m. and here I am, ready to at least try and do whatever bit of life today is about. Yesterday wasn't great and tomorrow might be worse and I've no idea how today's going to pan out, but I turned up then, I'll do it tomorrow and I'm here now, so let's crack on with things.

So even if I didn't and don't see the therapeutic benefit of drawing a tree, maybe it's one brick of the therapy that, if I pull it out, might make the rest start to collapse.

Whenever we knew a new person would be arriving, the place would turn into the yard of Shawshank Prison as we'd try to guess what they would be like. There were no bets placed – gambling in a rehab centre being frowned upon, of course – we'd just try to build a picture of what they would be like. They were often released on licence from prison so that would give you some idea of what you might get.

You'd speculate whether it was crack/booze/heroin, their age, their family, etc. 'OK, he'll be forty-nine, two kids, divorced, younger girlfriend who's in prison.' Like a Guess Who of failed lives. If newcomers knew this, it would probably put them off, but within a week they'd be speculating on whether a newcomer would have missing teeth or an aunt who lived in Carlisle.

Back in Focus, less-serious infractions had a three-strikes rule, and one of those was violence. You may think violence would trigger instant eviction and clearly if it was a serious enough incident, it would. But there was an understanding that they were dealing with very troubled people going through a very difficult and sometimes confrontational process, so a level of anger and violence in the proper context was understood if not tolerated.

More minor rule breaks would be read out in group session to keep track of where everyone was in terms of being on their first, second or third strike. Again, this fed back into the total honesty concept – nobody could pretend to be doing better than they were.

One person who fell foul of the one-strike rule on walking out of the therapy was a very successful person who wasn't allowed to have cartons of Um Bongo in his room, and when he was told this he kicked off so ferociously he chipped a tooth. He also walked out the building and we never saw him again. I often wonder whether he explained why his latest rehab failed because he loved apricot, guava & mango so much.

Graduation from rehab happened if you completed your course; it's not a pass or fail thing. There are projects you have to complete during that time (which are basically audits of where you are mentally and how you think you're doing, broadly following the steps of the 12 steps).

One issue I had was admitting the part where you say, I am powerless over my addiction. I think it's so badly worded. What they mean is, I can't have a single drink or a single line because I'm unable to leave it at that. I totally agree with that. But to say you're powerless isn't very . . . empowering. It took me a long time to come to terms with that.

People graduate even if, by the end, there are clear signs that they're not at the stage where they are ready to go sober. The after-care plan for people in this mindset would lean heavily towards addressing this, but ultimately the only person that can help them on the outside is themselves.

It's a really long course, which, if you commit to it, produces a lot of work. And I can absolutely say I worked fucking hard in Focus, even if a lot of it was on the back of a lie. And you learn a lot of background behaviours if you put the work in that stay with you. Like learning to drive a car, the unconscious behaviours are just there.

Quick tip. Make your bed in the morning. It might seem small and pointless, but if it's a day when you can do nothing else, you know you made your bed. And when you finally get to the point in the day you've been desperately waiting for, your bed looks all nice and comfy and lovely and you can be proud of it.

You've spent all day in a mess, don't climb into another one.

That was a really important lesson for me to learn. The way to be the sort of person who makes their bed, is to make your bed. Don't wait for the stars to align and a bright light to come down from the sky and announce you are cured and are now ready to enter society. Sometimes our actions can lead us where we need to go better than waiting for some mystic process to produce the action from inside to out. Eat breakfast. Open the curtains. Get there on time. Believe me, I am allergic to the fluffy wuffy side of mental health but, to my utter fucking surprise, this has massively helped me. If you wait to feel like the sort of person who does things like this, you never will. Every single person who does these things feels exactly as you do. You aren't some fundamentally broken human, you just haven't been given that particular cheat code.

Next Steps

I had completed the course and it was time for me to graduate. On the one hand I had worked my arse off, my mum and aunt were there, I had a nice turnout of patients and staff, and many people said very nice things. I had a real sense of pride. But on the other hand it was entirely based on a lie and I felt like I'd achieved nothing, as I'd drunk when I was doing panto and lied about it. I knew this process only works with 100 per cent honesty and, at the time, I felt it invalidated everything. I was sat, unable to take in all the nice things people were saying because a voice in my head knew I was lying.

I can see the value in the work I did now, but I couldn't then.

The graduation is just another therapy session, essentially. You don't get dressed up, and there's no ceremony; all you get is a little certificate to say you'd completed the course. I kept that certificate on my wall for a while but, every time I looked at it, I felt it was worthless because I'd been drinking, so it was just a piece of paper. If I stopped feeling bad about it, it would just be a free pass to excuse a load of future behaviour.

At my graduation, Jon, a therapist who'd gone through the programme himself and was 12 years clean, called me out on what he (correctly, as it turned out) felt was my bullshit. He bluntly stated that he thought I would fuck things up once I left Focus. He spent a good five minutes detailing how I would get things wrong and I realise now I should probably have asked him for lottery numbers while he was there because he predicted the future with startling accuracy.

He told me: You think you've got things sorted because you think you know more than everyone else (correct): you think you can do this in a different way because you know more than we do (correct); you think you have a different way but you don't and if you haven't listened to what we've said, you don't stand a chance (correct).

It wasn't that I hadn't put the work in during my stay; I can honestly say that I really had. Nor was it that I hadn't listened. For hours at a time in therapy, all you really can do is to listen. And a lot of the behaviours I learned during my time eventually became the way I now deal with life, one of which is being relentlessly honest even when it can sometimes be uncomfortable both for me and the person listening.

I had so many of the tools when I left rehab, I just think I wasn't ready to use them properly at that point. When I did get to the point where I was done and I was ready to start trusting myself, all the things I learned in Focus that I'd put in a box on a high shelf, I took down and started to use. Not in an actively conscious way, but clearly they were all there waiting for when I was ready to take them down.

I never took *illegal* drugs from the moment I arrived at Focus until the day I write this (and, I'm pretty confident in saying, any day after this). (You might have noticed that 'illegal' is doing quite a bit of heavy lifting. We'll come back to that a bit later.) Despite that, when I graduated, I felt like nothing had changed because I'd drunk during the therapy and I knew deep down I would drink the moment I was on my own long enough to do so. Mick had conceded defeat on the drugs but was adamant I was going to drink at the very least. So rehab had, in my head, failed.

It took a very long time to realise that Focus had tipped the balance towards me getting sober; it just took longer than I wanted it to. I'd wanted to walk out of there without drugs or alcohol in my life but I only got half the deal and I couldn't allow my addict brain to justify my drinking by celebrating the fact I was drug-free. I walked in an addict and walked out an addict, this was true. But something had changed. It would just take me a bit longer before I realised what it was.

I had thought I was at rock bottom when I entered Focus, but that was when I found that basement.

I'm very aware that when I write about experiencing emotions in an extreme way, it's dangerously close to those people who faux confess to feeling too deeply, or being unable to switch off their brain – brags disguised as flaws. But, trust me, it's shit.

The principle that your emotions and your thoughts aren't some unknowable kingdom, but that you can try and map them, has stayed with me from rehab. Someone once told me about a study that showed learning new names for emotions actually increases the range of emotions you can feel. If a child never learns that anger and frustration are separate feelings, they will think they are angry when they're frustrated. The fact that the Portuguese have a word, *saudade*, for an intense melancholic but almost pleasurable longing for something you can't have, actually means they experience those emotions differently.

Did I just google that last fact because I was struggling to find something interesting to say at the end of this chapter? Yes. But now we both know. You're welcome.

But in all seriousness, my emotional swings are one of the most destructive elements of my experience with BPD. I feel things wrong. I am in charge of my facts, Mick is in charge of my feelings.

One of the reasons Mick even exists – one of the reasons I dissociate my symptoms – is that it helps me to understand the difference between something that I'm feeling and something that I'm doing. It helps me sustain a level of everyday existence, in a world where I simply feel too much.

I can tell you what isn't sustainable though: holding down my feelings by never talking about them; going through life thinking that I exist without some fundamental thing that everyone else has; that my brain is so special and complicated that none of the other things that have worked for LITERALLY EVERYONE ELSE will work for me. That approach doesn't work.

Chapter Six

Unstable Relationships

A pattern of unstable and intense interpersonal relationships characterised by alternating between extremes of idealisation and devaluation

I don't have unstable relationships. The world's relationships with me all occur with the context of me being unstable. It's liking blaming the glasses when they fall over rather than the wobbly leg of the café table you're sat at. Or, more pertinently, imagine sitting at this wobbly table and a tank drives by and your drinks spill. You're probably not blaming the glasses or table for that.

In my relationships I'm the twat in the tank.

When you have all the stuff going on that I do, unstable relationships can feel like a by-product. But it's the intensity of those relationships and that aspect of idealisation and devaluation that are so intense that are key. I need my relationships to do things with an incredible intensity.

Of course, relationships aren't confined to romantic ones. We have relationships with family, with friends, with pets, and even objects like our car and our house that are completely separate from physical relationships. (If you have a physical relationship with an inanimate object, I'm obviously not judging.) I've got a relationship with my dog. I had a relationship with drugs. I still have a relationship with coffee.

At one point in my life I was regularly driving from Kent to Manchester and I would have a four-shot espresso at every service station I passed. I went back and worked it out recently. There are eight. That's 32 shots of espresso in three hours.

I derive a huge amount of my self-worth from work; it's a big relationship for me. It's incredibly intense and I can go from utter elation to despondency with startling speed. All these things are relationships, so they can all be unstable. The thing to remember is that relationships are made up of things you can control and things you can't. There's your bit of how you're behaving and, on one level, that's only ever half of the relationship. But if your behaviour is extreme then it starts to shape their behaviour and tips the scales so you have a disproportionate impact. If you're doing the emotional equivalent of setting fire to the duvet, it's not really fair to accuse the other person of being distant when they run out of the room.

I have to remember that Mick also always wants my relationships with people to fail because they're a barrier between me and loneliness. The end game is me on my own. Relationships are Mick's kryptonite, especially if I tell people he exists. If people know he's there he can't do anything.

My relationship with alcohol and drugs and work complicated my relationships with everything else. But they *really* mucked up my ability to have a functioning romantic relationship.

I am 28 years old and I have just finished singing an original song I wrote for my girlfriend, Sara, at her birthday party. In spite of the fact I am almost certain that we will split up. The song is full of reasons she is so great. As it ends and I look across at her expectant happy face and everyone in the audience's expectant happy faces and they start to get their phones out, I realise they think I am going to propose. There is silence that seems to last several hours, before people realise they'd better start clapping before things get even more awkward.

The thing is, I knew what the song sounded like and knew what people's reaction and expectations might be when a song like that gets sung. As the party approached, I had started to think that, knowing I planned to leave, maybe performing a song written for her wasn't a good idea. It might send out the wrong signals and, when I did leave, seem almost cruel.

Despite how deeply unhappy we were and how much worse things had been getting, I had pulled out all the stops for her birthday. Most people with one eye on the door would make no effort as they're not invested in the relationship. I put ten times the effort in that I would normally do, a magician's misdirection of 'Look over here at this great party' to distract from the widening cracks in the relationship.

When our relationship eventually fails, after three years, it will be because it was entirely built upon lies. My lies. It will be unable to sustain what I need it to, which is to utterly validate me as a person. Before we split up, she will help me fix my arm together with plastic strips, so I do not miss a moment of the pantomime I am in. I have cut myself to the tendon with a kitchen knife while falling down drunk. If that isn't the perfect image for what love looks like when you can only form unstable relationships, I don't know what is.

Dicks

Fair warning here. I'm going to start talking about sex. One of the main issues I have about that is that my girlfriend's mum and dad are going to be reading this. Sorry, Bob and Sue. I don't know which page to send you to, but just flick through about ten and you'll end up reading something that isn't *this*.

My sex drive is, ironically, fucked.

Sex is something I have rarely enjoyed throughout my life. I lost my virginity on a wicker sofa in a conservatory when I was 15 years old. It was exactly as comfortable as it sounds. I was so nervous I couldn't get hard so I, for want of a better phrase, tried to thumb in a softie, prompting her to loudly ask, 'Is it in yet?' (Seriously, Sue, if you're still here I desperately need you to move on.)

Even though that was my only sexual experience before moving to London for college, by the time I arrived I had fabricated a massive history of sexual exploits. Even now, I don't know how many people I've had sex with. Not because it's too many to count, but because I don't know how many people were made up back when I thought telling people about my sex life was a key to acceptance and making people like me.

When I was using, I went through a stage where I was around prostitutes regularly. And by regularly, I mean every week. But because I was sleep deprived, effectively starving, and on copious amounts of coke, it wasn't about sex. I'd just keep paying them to keep me company so I wasn't on my own. They were fucking expensive chats.

Right from the beginning, my first sexual encounters had come about enmeshed in lies. At the ice rink, I was a

15-year-old pretending to be a 21-year-old with the end result that I appeared to be an excitingly older guy. At college, I had a sexual history to die for. Ironic that.

At stage school, there was a general lack of prudishness about sex. You don't have to quickly undress in front of each other twice a night if you're an accountant and you're seldom called upon to kiss each other or pretend to shag.

You have people who've known each other for five years through stage school from the age of 12. Child performers are treated as adults, making you feel older than you are, and this makes it more likely to happen. It feels like part of the adult world that you're about to be part of.

I don't think people talk about sex enough. Especially men. I mean they talk about it, in a kind of performative, who's the best fictional shagger way, but not properly. The leading cause of death for men under 45 is suicide. I refuse to believe a significant number of those deaths aren't caused by both an inability, and a lack of outlets, to talk properly about sex and how it makes us feel, how much of our value is defined by our ability to have it, and how twisted and poisonous the narratives that lead someone to believe it is their right can become. As someone so brilliantly once put it, women are not vending machines into which you put friendship until the sex comes out.

There are no statistics on this subject because nobody talks about it. It's a self-contained, potentially fatal loop of silence.

For example, where is it that we're supposed to talk about the size of our dicks?

The scariest place I ever go is a urinal. I've not seen many other dicks in my time. I've seen a lot of mine. I think its fine – nothing compared to the Shetland pony in rehab, I'll give you that, but not too bad.

That's a lie. I don't think it's fine at all. I can't bear the thought of having sex because I can't bear the thought of being naked, even when I'm alone. If there's the prospect of being naked with another person, now that I'm in a relationship, it's because I care about them deeply. The last thing I want to do is make them look at me.

I've watched a lot of porn. Nobody's got a small dick in porn. I'm not watching porn for the dicks. If I'm honest, when I have watched porn and seen someone with a dick the size of mine, I've moved on.

So much of who I am and what I think is tied up in the size of something nobody ever sees. I don't know if it's because I didn't have that many friends when I grew up, or because I never played football, but I never had much chance of knowing if I'm normal. I don't think football players sword-fight with each other as they have a whazz, but they at least have an idea of what someone else's dick looks like without watching porn.

I was diagnosed with PTSD recently because the hundreds of hours I spent high watching porn and certain I was about to be murdered have for ever linked sexual desire and intense fear.

This is the first time I've told anybody this, and the fact that I'm telling you in a place where you can't tell me how you're responding is no accident. I don't need someone else to tell me I'm not enough. I mean, you're reading this, you already know that I feel that most of the time.

Penis enlargements should be a more common thing.

Nobody talks about getting their dick enlarged. Yet boob jobs are fine. Why is that? Yet I've never heard anybody talking about cocks being enlarged anywhere but in my spam folder. I've googled it more than once, but I've got no way of factoring in whether or not the surgeons offering it are good at what they do. It feels like too much of a risk.

I'm going to move on because I'm 34 and, even though this is the first time I've had this chat, it's been more than enough. First time I've ever felt like I've been enough during sex, ironically. I just want you to know that I'm unhappy about something I can't change.

I don't know who you are: you might be somebody that feels like me. But you also might be somebody that has loved somebody like me. Please know that it's not you. To love somebody that feels like me can make you feel unwanted, unattractive or worthless.

You are not.

For years, I thought in order to wank you had to be completely naked. Socks-off naked. Not-even-wearing-a-hat naked. Didn't matter where or when – and I was a 15-year-old boy remember, so the world was my wank oyster – if it was go-time, I would get completely naked before I started. Who are you supposed to have that conversation with? And let's remember this is entirely before other people have even got involved in a sex act.

For those who are interested, this is how I found out:

Me: It's a nuisance when you're out and about and fancy one and have to take your socks off, innit?

Older boy: Yeah, I know what you mean . . . Wait, *what*?

Me: What?

These conversations have no place, especially in adult life. There's no environment for them. There's Sex Addicts Anonymous but nobody is going there to say how bad they are at it. They're the worst meetings to go to because you know somebody there is going to try and fuck you.

This is the right time for another bit of content warning – there's a brief chat about sexual assault over the next couple of pages. If this isn't for you, turn to page 142. I can't promise it's that cheerful, but there's at least nothing that will harm you in that bit. But I'll give you a hug through the pages as you flip them.

Being touched sexually is probably one of the quickest ways to make me think I need to kill myself. If I'm touched in that way, it's like my blood turns into ice water and my body retracts into itself. It's quite an extreme reaction, and it hasn't always been that way.

Years ago, when I was in my early twenties, I was out with a group of friends. They weren't people I was particularly close with, but they were a perfectly nice bunch.

There was one guy, whose name was Richard. I didn't really know him, but we caught up like old mates. We'd all been out drinking, heavily of course, and went back to his place. After a few hours everybody started to leave, and I got my head down ready to sleep on the floor. I was the only one left.

In the early hours, I woke up and felt somebody's hand moving around in my pants. I felt sick but just assumed I was still dreaming. As I came to a bit more, I could see out of the corner of my eye that it was Richard. He'd come down-stairs, got under the duvet, and this was actually happening.

I froze. Didn't move, didn't say anything, just stayed there, still, pretending to sleep. I remember wishing that I'd actually throw up because it might stop him. I didn't have an erection at this point (I did when I first woke up, because I was asleep when he started. That's always been a large part of the shame I have attached to this) but he carried on regardless for the next few minutes. Then he just stopped and rolled over.

I stood up, as silent as I could be, picked up my clothes from the couch, and calmly walked to the front door. I didn't even put my shoes on. I went outside and stood in the middle of the residential road on a freezing January night in my pants and called a cab.

I didn't cry. I still haven't cried. Over the years I've been very flippant about this happening. You're the only person I've told that isn't my mum and my girlfriend. I never brought it up in any of the rehabs I've been to or with my psychiatrist.

Yet I've always had copious amounts of shame around it, while at the same time never really felt that it was a problem, because it falls into the dissociation category. I didn't feel it, and I don't feel it, in order to cope with it.

But every time somebody else touches me, the memory of utter fear and disgust I had that night comes hurtling back to me. It's been over a decade. That's a problem.

For me, sex, and my various mishaps within its world, have all been amplified to the point of distortion by self-loathing. I've never really talked about it because you're not meant to. I know how close to self-destruction my thoughts about sex have led me, I know how talking about other subjects have pulled me away from suicide and I still can't talk about it easily. Not having sex, not feeling like you deserve to have sex, being repulsed by the thought of yourself having sex and being convinced that when it does happen, you are terrible at it.

When you have the level of self-loathing that I do, sex is very difficult because I don't want to have sex where somebody like me is involved. So somebody else's willingness to join in is baffling. It's got worse as I've got older because I've become more self-aware and therefore more aware of how much this bothers me. I no longer have alcohol or drugs to push those thoughts aside, either.

The options society gives you are: lie about it; or don't talk about it at all. Both behaviours push me towards killing myself.

Throughout my life, my intimate relationships have been a battleground that Mick has had enormous success with. He knows that sex is a subject I find very difficult to talk about. So he knew that constantly conjuring images of my girlfriend having sex with her ex would work an absolute treat because my usual solution – talk sunlight onto his dark thoughts until they go away – would be a bigger challenge than usual.

Not just images, though. When you walk into a department store and go to the TV section and they have every kind of screen from a little tablet to a home cinema system all showing the same thing. When there's countless screens visible from every angle and for some reason the staff have decided to turn the sound up to full volume. Those kind of images.

Mick knows that I ask her about the things he tells me and she reassures me they're not true and then the power they have goes away. He also knows I can't do this with the multiscreen surround-sound sex show. Because he's learned the subjects I find it hardest to talk about.

This is how Mick gets his feedback loop. Self-loathing makes sex fraught. Fraught sex feeds feelings of self-loathing. Feelings of validation come from relationships. Being a bit weird about sex is a silent problem in a relationship that creates self-loathing. Rinse and repeat.

This is a background noise to everything else.

Exit Wound

When I left Focus, I moved into a large, light-filled flat in a different neighbourhood to the flat where souls go to die. Close to work and, importantly, locations for rehab meetings. It was part of my release plan arranged with Focus and my family. I went along with this, enthusiastically saying how ideal the location was, especially its proximity to rehab meetings, but I knew realistically I had no intention of going to any of them.

Part of the exit strategy is to have a plan for what each day will look like so there are no empty gaps that could be filled with relapse.

In my exit plan, I assumed I would be filming anywhere between four to twelve hours a day.

You're expected to leave rehab with a degree of confidence, or at least a faked degree of confidence. You sort of have to. And so, faking it, I went in to work. When I got there, they told me that the writers would start the process of writing me back into the show, which had a two-month lead time, given how far ahead serial television has to plan.

This meant I went to a diary full of events to a diary full of nothing. I thought when I told them I'd be back in two months' time, they'd start the process then. When I left Fancy Rehab I had started work the next day. But not now. What I should have done is immediately contact my support network and tell them I had large open vistas of empty space that addiction couldn't wait to fill in. That's what I should have done. What I actually did was tell nobody. Because I still wasn't in the business of making my life easy for myself.

It doesn't take a lot of convincing for an addict's brain in that situation to say, 'Well, you might as well start drinking. That's a good idea.' It wasn't like I was going to meetings to have to tell people that was a decision I'd made. And it wasn't like I was using my contact network to let them know. You're responsible for your own recovery so it's not other people's job to ask whether network television schedules have jeopardised your rehab. You're meant to proactively call them and let them know.

I did have my sponsor but, again, it was up to me to call him if I needed help, rather than him calling me to see how things were going, and there was no way I was going to make that call, partially because I'd rationalised myself into thinking I didn't need to. I did keep in touch with him but I wasn't telling him the truth, so it was a pretty pointless exercise. He would sometimes ask about meetings but I'd be non-committal enough to deflect the question.

I drank in the flat from the day I moved in. It's depressing to admit there weren't days of writhing on my bed, gnashing my teeth as I battled in vain against my addiction demons, but there weren't. I did a little food shop without booze and took it back to the flat. Ate that. Sat around bored for a bit. Went for a walk away from shops and looked at the river. Lovely. Came back to the flat. That killed four hours and I'd exhausted what I thought were my available diversions. May as well go and get some booze, I thought. I was actually angry because I hate walking and I felt I'd wasted four hours when I could have just bought the drink straight away.

When I drank during panto, I could rationalise that I was drinking in pubs, socially, with friends. OK, I was drinking three drinks to their one and I wasn't meant to be drinking at all, but come on, this wasn't *problem drinking*. All nonsense, but a lie I could tell myself. Buying bottles of booze to take back to an empty flat robs you even of that option.

A litre of vodka would last two days but I was adding mixers and ice and drinking from a clean glass so it still possibly sort of wasn't maybe problem drinking a bit, do you see? As an addict there's always somebody you can look down on, even if it's the difference between buying upmarket booze and supermarket brand or adding a splash of diet coke.

Alcoholism removes the pretence that you do it for the taste, not that I ever really liked the taste anyway. I met a high-flying exec in rehab who bought perfume on long-haul flights to keep his alcohol levels topped up and not because Chanel No. 5 goes well with a dash of tonic water. He may have drunk a £100 bottle of wine in the airport and got a £25 cocktail when he got to his hotel, but when perfume and hand sanitiser is all that's available, that will do. No matter who you are, you're all heading to the same point.

Being the show it is, a few months away from the soap opera meant that a third of the cast I knew had died in the show from a mixture of serial killers, wobbly ladders and helicopter incidents. But I knew that a guy from a previous job had started on the show so I got in touch with him. And while we're still very good friends, in the beginning I was using him as a way to drink.

We arranged to meet up because rehab tells you that sitting on your own will kill you. So meeting up with him was a way of sticking to the programme. If I hadn't then gone drinking with him, that may almost have made sense. As somebody who knew nothing of my backstory he was perfect, because I could engage in whatever level of drinking I chose to tell him – as a young guy who didn't know much about rehab – was OK. I told him I did drug rehab, not drink rehab, so let's have a pint. He had no reason to believe this was bullshit.

This shows the lack of a long game plan I had. I knew he worked on the show, I knew I'd be back at work soon, logic dictated that he'd mention we'd been out drinking at some point, but those would be reasonable moments of foresight somebody who hadn't spent their life assuming they're going to die soon would have.

This guy and I got on immediately, but on our first night out, I was unconsciously checking him to see what I could and couldn't tell him. He's a lovely bloke and very trusting so initially this was a lot. The mask soon slips in situations like this, because there's a time limit to how long you can maintain things. It's 3 p.m. on a Wednesday, they're nursing a pint and you're slumped in the toilets covered in your own shit. Stuff like that stands out. An excessive drinker or coke addict quickly changes from the person you did that massive session with to that person you had that awful night with where you went home a bit terrified. I think I may have scared straight a number of people by way of being a four-dimensional public information film.

I would have people come to visit me, but the length of their visit was always predicated on how long I could stay sober while they were there. Anything over a couple of days wasn't an option. And having visitors seeing me apparently sober was money in the bank, as they could report back to friends and family that I was doing fine. I took a photo of me and Dad on my sofa to show how well I was doing and sent it to Chip. He replied, 'Recovery goals.'

No, it wasn't.

Ultimately, I was protecting the drink because that was the thing that mattered most. I've done over four months of rehab; if I couldn't stop then I never would. Sorry family/friends/work but I have to protect the thing I do. This was my main motivation. Sara moved to a different city to live and because almost the entirety of our conversations happened when I was in various degrees of off my face, I wasn't *entirely* sure if we were a couple or not. I kept her in the loop of lies by text message just in case.

The longer I could delay people finding out, the better, and I honestly thought that moment could last for ever. I could make this OK. Unlike everyone else ever. I was unplugged from the rationality of the situation but I now know this was Mick, just another symptom of my BPD trying to find a way to kill me. I didn't have a secret room with diagrams and flow charts, just a mental checklist of convenient lies, deceptions that would do for now and no plan for the future. There was no intention to hurt anyone but myself. As much as I know I was lying to others I knew it came from my BPD's need to keep me lying to myself.

The two months' drinking without work taught me how to drink a lot, very quickly. My volume increased massively. I never got to the physical addiction symptoms stage but they would have arrived eventually. But, as with the drugs, the timetable was planned around being able to function at work. I told myself that I wasn't doing drugs any more, so things could be worse. This was a level of ignorance rehab had repeatedly told me I couldn't afford and couldn't pretend to have. I knew. I *knew*. I was drunk all the time, even when I wasn't drunk. At no point was alcohol not in my system.

My first day back at the studio went without fanfare. It's a busy workplace like any other. There was a lot of new cast members who had no idea who I was and my personality isn't the type to impose myself in the green room to say hello. Even regular cast members who I'd never had scenes with might not really know me, because the show would often have distinct character groups who never overlapped. This helped me in keeping my secrets going, but the production team knew what had been going on. Or at least as much as I had told them, which was whatever I thought they needed to hear for me to keep drinking.

I had a meeting with the producers, but they could only help me as much as I wanted help and, at that moment, I wasn't the best person to ask what help I needed.

My lies had increased massively once I got back to work. I was a sweaty mess and all over the place. As well as the drink, I was still on a maraca's worth of pills every day to deal with my mental health and I'd ballooned in weight compared to when I went into Focus. I was carrying around an aniseed-flavoured bowling ball of Sambuca waste on my stomach and looked like a middle-aged man towards the end of his tether. But people equate addiction with being skinny, so chubby Joe must be doing better, they thought. I was lying to my family, lying to Sara and everyone else around me.

People would ask how I was doing and, as per the social contract, I'd say I was fine. Then there was the follow-up question of how I was *really* doing, usually with a head tilt and a concerned look.

There was always going to come a point when continuing to drink and continuing to work was going to stop being possible and eventually my work started to suffer. This wasn't immediately noticeable to others, but I knew that my ways of working were becoming increasingly impossible to maintain. I knew I wasn't performing as well as I was capable of, even when I was permanently high.

The drink was the only thing I was interested in protecting, so there was nothing I could do about it but keep going until . . . what?

As an actor, I never learn my lines until shortly before filming. In the sort of show I was working on, when you're doing multiple scenes that are often out of sequence and often don't relate to each other, there's no point in retaining big chunks of dialogue. The quicker you can learn it, the quicker you can forget it and move on to the next bit.

The drink was affecting my ability to do this unconsciously, as I'd always done before. It became a conscious process and if you've ever walked up stairs and started thinking about how you walk up stairs, you'll recognise the change it makes and how awkward it becomes. As soon as I was thinking about it, it stopped working.

And I had no plan B, because plan B would almost certainly have to involve not drinking. I just wasn't on it, and I knew it and eventually so did they.

After a disagreement with the producers, I got home that night, downed half a bottle of Sambuca and tweeted that I was going to leave the show when my contract ended. Announcing it in this way was deliberately irrevocable, like copying everyone into a work email that your boss can shove his job up his arse. I had managed two years of alcoholism and working but if one had to go, I knew which one it had to be.

It was into this context that my relationship with Sara came. Like everyone else, she'd assumed I was sober because that's what I'd told her.

Work had failed to be The Thing that would stop me drinking so my relationship with Sara became The Thing instead. This is what would save me from myself. She was happy to join in project Make Me Feel Better without knowing alcohol was part of that. She'd recently split up with her ex who still wanted her back, and, for somebody with zero self-esteem, that's a hard thing to deal with. Why not him rather than me? Also, pretending to be sober when you're busy filming and not spending all your time together is a lot easier than when you have somebody around you most of the time. But I did want to stop drinking, I hated lying and was kind of bored of feeling like I was going to die all the time.

As usual, I jumped into the relationship with something bordering on obsession. If I was texting her, that was the only thing that mattered in the world, even if I was at work. So, without work, she was my whole focus.

The day she said we were a full-time couple I stopped the cab home from work at an off-licence where I bought half a litre of vodka. This would have been mid-afternoon. I drank the whole bottle in the seven minutes I had left between the off-licence and home. That was not a way of drinking I'd done since my journey to court and there was no rational thought involved. I couldn't drink at work and I couldn't drink at home, because I knew Sara was there waiting for me. I had a 20-minute window to drink and I used it.

When I got out of the cab, I wasn't drunk, but, within ten minutes, I was very clearly and visibly hammered. I denied that I'd been drinking to her a few times, as best as I could with half a litre of vodka in me that hadn't even got up to body temperature yet, but I know I'm not that good an actor. Nobody is.

I was indisputably drunk and I had no option but to tell her, and to also tell her that I'd been drinking all along. If I was going to invest in Sara as the thing that fixed me, she needed to know what she was fixing. To an extent, it was a way of revealing this in a way I couldn't turn back. I say this with a perspective I have now that I didn't have then.

At some point I passed out. She stayed with me that night and in the morning called her ex who was an alcoholic in recovery. Not to change her decision on boyfriends, simply because she was unequipped to deal with a lapsed alcoholic and needed advice. She then called my dad and it was agreed that he would come and stay with me. Looking back, I am aware of how immensely lucky I have been that people stayed in my life, but when you're an alcoholic the last thing you want is someone getting in the way of you drinking.

The process of how to write me out of the show had now started. As an actor you have no input into this. At the time I saw this as them not knowing how to make the best use of my talents. Now I can see I wasn't easy to work with due to the drinking.

Dad arrived to stay with me. Because everyone assumed I'd been going to meetings and because everyone assumed going to meetings was the only way to make this right, I was once more taken to meetings. Whether I wanted to or not was beside the point. I'd messed up and had to accept the consequences that came along with the support.

Dad took me to one the same day he arrived. At the end of a meeting, there's time for a new arrival to introduce themselves, which at this meeting obviously included me. I had nothing to tell them. The only honest thought I could express was, 'All I can think about is that my dad is back at the flat having sex with my girlfriend right now. That's all I've got.'

I knew that this wasn't likely to be happening but this didn't dislodge the thought. I was aware of how odd a thought it was and was possibly the first time I'd noticed that there was somebody in my head trying to tell me the worst things possible, to get me to think about things that would take me to the darkest possible place. Though he wouldn't get identified and named for a while, Mick was in there, doing some light stretches, limbering up.

Following that meeting, I had a couple of weeks with just me and Dad in the flat, with texts/calls to Sara. She hadn't *left me*, left me, but my various and obvious lapses had reset the trust counter in our relationship to zero.

I'd also contacted my sponsor to be honest about what I'd actually been doing. It wouldn't have been a shock for him to receive the call – most people in recovery relapse and as a sponsor, it's a golden opportunity to hear about how fucked up addiction makes you, a thing rehab says you need constantly reminding of to keep you straight. Every terrible thing your relapsed sponsor buddy tells you ticks off your recovery bingo card. 'Lost your house? Tick. Crashed the car? Tick.'

It's a two-way street. In recovery, calling a sponsor is a chance to show what a recovered person looks like, that the system can work and that here is a shining example of hope on the other end of the phone. And the longer you've stayed clean, the more cache your sobriety has. A one-week-sober addict is like somebody who ran out of the reception of the World Trade Center whereas somebody 30 years sober is like somebody who managed to get out from the 74th floor.

I told my sponsor everything I'd done because whenever I get caught doing something, I always confess *everything* I've done, as well as some other stuff I did that might not be related but I should tell you anyway. Aged 12 I worked in a magic shop and stole some nudey playing cards. My criminal genius brain knew the shop had CCTV, so I waited until the monitor wasn't showing the section of the shop with the cards before pocketing them. Being a 12-year-old, it didn't occur to me that when it's not on the monitor it's STILL RECORDING.

As soon as I was rumbled a total apology and explanation spilled out of me, no attempt at denial even considered. I've never wanted to be a liar, which I know has often not stopped me. It takes such energy to lie, so when you have that window of opportunity to unload the heavy backpack of dishonesty you've been carrying around, you take it.

People could only accompany me to meetings for so long and, as soon as I was trusted to make my own way there, I stopped going. I didn't start drinking, I just stopped going to meetings. I didn't stop leaving the flat because I had to be seen going *somewhere*. So I'd get a cab to a shopping centre instead. Paranoid that somebody I knew would see me there, tell Sara and my non-attendance be found out, I'd hide in the car park until it was time to go home again.

Sara was strict about what I ate, understandably, as I am a fussy eater whose pickiness doesn't run to healthy options. So while I sat hiding in a car park, I would stuff my face with the Tangfastics and Gummi Bears that I wasn't allowed at home. I looked forward to meetings not for the shot at redemption but for the shot at some E-numbers.

This was the same impulse as drinking in the back of the taxi. Here was a narrow window to behave self-destructively, and I took it. Without thought about why I was doing it or what the plan was. All I knew was that hiding in a shopping centre ruining my teeth was better than going to meetings or telling everyone I wasn't going to them.

My last two weeks of filming had all this going on in the background. Once I'd finished, I could work entirely on my relationship with Sara from a level of no trust whatsoever, which is not a great starting place. But I managed to convince her that this is what I needed, this would be the thing that allowed me to be the person I needed to be to deserve her love.

I quickly moved in with her while keeping my flat in a different city. I needed that flat as a place in which to sit quietly not existing. I now realise that Mick needed that flat as an isolated place so he could have me to himself to go to town on me, even though I never ended up using it.

I cared deeply for Sara and I genuinely felt the relationship could make the difference to my sobriety but I do know I spent almost all of this period of my life telling Mum I wanted to end it. I can see now I had only really been in one relationship my whole life and that was with Mick. I was cheating on him with her and moving in with her was reducing him to the role of a mistress.

I still found ways to drink while living with Sara, but it was limited to opportunity. It wasn't the daily obliteration of old, I would have periods of six to eight weeks I'd stay sober, but then I'd have a binge event and be right back at alcoholic levels of drinking.

Next Steps

My first job after the soap opera was working in a play with my dad.

I did a couple of weeks' rehearsal, we had a week off, and the run was due to start in Liverpool. Most of the rehearsals took place without Dad but he was still there a lot and we were doing multiple TV appearances to promote the show, so I was around him a lot, which was never my most comfortable place to be. Me being around Dad wasn't comfortable for other people, either.

The night before the first show, Dad stayed in mine and Sara's flat so we could travel together to Liverpool the following morning. By 10.30 a.m. he still wasn't out of bed so I knocked on the spare room door to see how he was doing. How he was doing was sat wrapped in the duvet, shivering and asking if it was cold. It wasn't and we had a show to get to, so he got himself together and we drove to Liverpool with me internally fuming that this was another example of him not allowing me to have anything – like an opening night at a show – to myself. It wouldn't be out of the ordinary for him to pull something like this.

But when at the theatre I went to his dressing room and found him lying face down on the floor. He asked me to get him some food, presumably hoping a Tesco sandwich might turn things around, so I went to get some, but by the time I got back he was already on the way to hospital.

Things were clearly very serious. This was Dad's first day off in 30 years. (I in no way want to put the blame for my brain back a generation in too simplistic a way. But I'm just saying that maybe that's quite a good example of someone having a very intense relationship with work. I'm just leaving that here.)

Of course, a parent who might die is not a good enough reason not to do a show, so I completed final rehearsals and did that night's show. It was a given for all concerned – me, the theatre company and (had he been well enough to say this) my dad.

Afterwards, when I saw him in the hospital, he was as ill as I'd ever seen him. He remained in hospital for a week before returning to work, drastically early and very much against medical advice. Doctors told him he needed three weeks' recovery at least and wouldn't get better while he continued to work. This was ignored by Dad despite the doctors being absolutely spot on with their prognosis. This kind of reckless approach to your own health didn't even raise an eyebrow at work because it's the kind of thing you just do.

It was the first time I'd worked with Dad for any length of time since I was a kid. While there was the temptation to fall back into the old habits of our old working relationship, I did start to work out new ways of us co-existing. His week in hospital made me see that I needed to change the way we were together, because the current way wasn't working. For me, at least.

Sara had to go away for a few days. While she was on the other side of the world, as I was texting her to see how she was doing, my brain saw the chance to get rid of her. I could drink, she was half a planet away, it would be fine. Knowing full well that half a bottle of spirits very quickly affects me and my ability to text coherently. Sara might not have been able to smell my breath but she would notice when my texts starting looking like I'd sat on my phone. Maybe this time it will be enough to make her leave.

My only options the next day when Sara inevitably confronted me on my drinking were total honesty or total denial and I chose total denial. She told me we could work through it if I told the truth and I chose not to anyway. I'd been conditioned to believe honesty about emotions was bad and offers of help weren't sincere so that was my frame of reference.

My pattern of drinking – weeks of abstinence followed by short, intense bouts of drinking – wasn't common for an alcoholic. My theory now is that this was because it was Mick that was an alcoholic and it was his cravings that I caved into. I'd never wanted to drink, it was always Mick and his tantrums that had led to it happening. At this point in my life, I was learning to ignore the tantrums and they were becoming less frequent as they became less successful.

I was staying sober for long bouts but only on the surface. I knew I was going to drink again eventually. You're not sober in between your trips to the bar, even if the gaps between those trips are months.

Sara's getting back coincided with me clearing out my flat ahead of the contract ending and me moving all my stuff into her place. As you do when you move home, you take the opportunity to throw stuff out. Sara used the opportunity to throw out several thousand pounds' worth of clothes of mine that she didn't like and I did. Rather than protesting, I used the approach I'd grown up with, of not putting forward an argument and, three days later, holding onto the resentment when I can't do anything with it.

None More for the Road

My last drink coincided with my last trip to a casino. With the flat empty, Sara went back to Manchester and I stayed behind to finish up. 'Finish up' very quickly became drinking very heavily that day. More drunk messages to Sara followed, setting up another appointment with The Talk the next day.

I had £200 to my name at the time. The play aside, I'd not worked for a while and was largely living via Sara's cash card and the occasional family loan. I decided I needed £800. What I needed it for, I have no idea. But I needed to go to the casino to make that happen.

I went to the casino, changed the £200 into chips and headed to the nearest roulette table without pausing for a second. I put all £200 on black and watched the wheel spin, spin, spin and land on black. No elation, no surprise, I just knew I now had £400. I moved it over to red and the wheel spun again. This time landing on red. My £200 was now £800 and I can't have been in the building more than five minutes.

I took my winnings, went back to the same cashier I'd seen when I arrived, and changed the chips into the £800 I needed. If this was a higher power teaching me about the evils of gambling, it was a really weird lesson. If the plan was to give me an unrealistic example of what gambling is like, it didn't work, as I never gambled in a casino again. All it did was, for a few minutes, make me look cool as fuck.

The reason it was my last casino visit was because it was the last time I drank. The drink would unlock the self-destruct option of gambling, so without the drink, it ceased to be an option in the first place. I got a cab home with the £800.

I drove to Manchester the following day to meet Sara and to have The Talk. I told her sincerely – it was always sincere, even when I failed – that I was sorry and I would never drink again. I didn't know that this time I actually wouldn't. Sara certainly didn't know and had no reason to suspect otherwise, given my track record. Life doesn't give you a fanfare to make you pay attention; you only know it's a huge moment when life proves it to be a huge moment.

But sat in my car, outside the gym where I'd driven to meet her, I said to her, 'I will never drink alcohol again', and for the first time in my life I made that promise to myself and others and I stuck to it.

OK, sort of. I was on my way to see *The Rocky Horror Show*, six months after my official first day of being sober. I was thinking about drinking because alcoholics are always thinking about drinking. When I was drinking I'd always placed significance on having that first single drink because I felt it would light up every nerve ending in my body. My face would go red and I'd start sweating because I attached so much to the action of drinking. So walking through Covent Garden I suddenly decided: 'Fuck it, I'm having a glass of champagne.' I went to a basement bar and ordered a glass. I drank half of it in one go and I remember saying out loud 'NO.' I threw the glass against the wall, a gesture so feeble I didn't even manage to smash the champagne flute. I went about my day and have never drunk since then.

I would remain sober. Which is when my problems really got started.

One of the major realisations I had was that my relationship with drugs and alcohol was just one of the unhealthy relationships I had with all sorts of things – people, my job, food.

The problem was the relationship, not the thing. I mean, I guess if you're just really addicted to eating carrot sticks, that's objectively better than crystal meth, but I bet there are people who have swapped in one for the other. You can have an obsessive relationship with scrolling on your phone. A good rule for me has become asking why I need this thing to be what it is. What is the crushing weight I am putting on this thing, what do I need it to fix about me?

Mick had spent over a decade suggesting drugs and alcohol as a way of trying to kill me and, even when I stopped listening to the drugs suggestion, I kept letting him have the alcohol. But a combination of circumstances made him realise that it wasn't going to work any more.

My inspirational 'hallelujah, now-my-life-changes' moment was quite simply that Mick got bored telling me to drink because it had stopped working so well. Like a toddler who stops bashing his palms against the door of the cupboard with the bleach in, Mick finally gave up.

I don't want to give him all the credit. I'd done the work in rehab stints, even if they'd not entirely stuck and even if I had resisted some of their lessons. The ways of thinking were there for me to use, even if they took a while to stick. I had wanted to change my life and, when I had failed, I had tried again. And by successfully quitting drugs and isolating my drinking to short bursts, I had shown Mick that I was capable of sobriety. (The anniversary of my becoming sober is the 15th of March, in case you were interested. Please don't send wine. That said, because of the champagne technicality, Mick can't resist a little dig every time the date rolls around. *You're not technically seven years sober, are you?*) I had made my life as difficult as possible for him to continue and everything had lined up to give me the best chance to not drink. Yes, he had got bored, but only because I had done everything I could to keep that cupboard door shut. I maximised the possibility of him giving up and he finally did.

That wouldn't have happened until I opened up a window and let light in on what was going on in my head. Through the tools that therapy had given me, through reframing the relationships I had with everything else in the world, I was able to put away another one of the bits of scaffolding I had been using to prop the sagging building of me up.

Chapter Seven

Explosive Anger

Inappropriate, intense anger or difficulty controlling anger

Imagine Bruce Banner was a bit short and wore glasses. And instead of turning into a large green monster that destroyed an entire city, he just called his uncle a cunt in Morrison's.

I didn't use to consider myself to be an angry person because I seldom directed my anger outwards. Then I thought about how often and how furiously angry I am with myself on an hourly basis and had to revise that assessment. Anger is far easier to recognise when it's being used against somebody else, rather than inwardly as part of an ongoing dialogue of self-loathing.

I go through life desperately trying not to get angry. It's a primal, childlike state where we're unable to process the anger rationally. You've seen a toddler when they're in a temper tantrum. A tiny boat tossed on a sea of rage. Completely unable to control the enormous feeling – there is nothing there but anger. And then it passes.

And afterwards, Banner and I know we did some bad stuff but our memories of it are a bit vague. He lies in the rubble of the building he destroyed wondering how he got there and why his trousers are still intact. I come round in an Aldi car park wondering why my hand is bleeding and whether my relationship is still intact.

On balance it's the symptom I experience the least, which is a good thing. But because of that, it's the symptom I've got the least knowledge of how to manage, which is a bad thing. Because when it does come along, the thing is, it feels like an appropriate level of anger. If someone else sees me screaming at a text, I'll be able to tell from their reaction that wasn't OK. But when I scream at my phone on my own, I've no insight into how angry I get.

And it feels very binary, like the Hulk. There's no half measures. It's not like one of his hands goes a bit green. He's either not there or the Hulk. It's a manipulative tool Mick uses because I try not to be angry but when I do get angry and come back to me, I think, 'Fuck, what did I do? What did I say?' And that's intentional, it's by design. Because then in the aftermath of the anger comes the recrimination, the self-loathing and the guilt.

But BPD is an illness that tries to convince you you've not got it. Ironically, Mick doesn't believe in mental health problems. He tells me I do stuff for attention. With the anger, it doesn't sit well with me, it never has.

It was the first thing to bubble to the surface as the frozen lake that had been my brain on booze and drugs began to thaw in those early months. It was the first toy Mick chose to play with, but there would be many more.

I am 28 years old and I am screaming incoherently in a rabbit onesie. As I try and yank it off, I am pulling and pulling and wordlessly screaming, feeling the material rip, until I realise it isn't the material, it's the skin of my chest and I am unzipping myself. Sara stares at me in absolute horror, though looking back I have a suspicion this may have been tempered somewhat by the fact I am wearing a rabbit onesie.

Sara and I have been living together while I am learning to live sober for the last six months. This is not the first time I have become overcome with anger. It will transpire afterwards that she thought I just loved arguments, but I think I have a child's brain, with no emotional regulation, who saw arguments as the only way of dealing with things.

Looking back, I can see I was angry at my life or rather my lack of life. I wasn't drinking. I hadn't worked since the play with my dad. When your life has been a knot of work and addiction, and you take away both, it leaves a big hole to fill and I didn't know how to be. Just – to be. So I was dealing with it as an adolescent. I was either fine or incandescently angry.

Part of total sobriety has required me being the same person in every room, with every person and in every situation. Consistently me, whatever 'me' has turned out to be. The convoluted spider webs of different lies told to different people, of remembering what level of drink and drugs I was allowed to be on, had gone. To be a better person, I had to be the same person in every room I walked into.

Looking back, it's hard to see what I spent my time doing. I was learning to spend time with just me for the first time in years. This involved spending a lot of time on the internet. I also recreated every song from Eurovision that year.

I was still seeing my Sharpie-haired psychiatrist at the time. When I was using, there was little he could do to help because all his information about my life came from me, via whatever new lies I brought to him that session. But now I was sober, we were still speaking about some of the same patterns of behaviour, only now without drink or drugs involved.

So one day I asked whether the way I felt was a recognised thing. He confirmed it was but was also reluctant to tell me what it was. I now know he knew me well enough that if I had a name for a condition with symptoms listed, there was a chance I'd research it then manipulate the symptoms to my own advantage. I'd done that often enough as an addict – knowing the symptoms and behaviours well enough to use them as they suited me.

Nevertheless he confirmed that he'd long suspected I'd had Borderline Personality Disorder but had been unable to confirm that while the drugs and alcohol sat over the top of the symptoms. My recent sobriety was enough for him to be sure.

BPD. I had BPD. There we go, all the chaos in my head had three letters to explain what caused it. He showed me the main symptoms and they were essentially a clinical diary of my life. I'd always thought I was the only person in the world who was this mental but reading this meant that enough people were like this that it was diagnosable. When I was uniquely mental, I was unfixable. But this was a thing, and a thing can be fixed.

I called Sara that night to tell her I now had three letters after my name. Not as distinguished as an MBE or as irritating as STD but three letters that might explain things.

Five to 15 years of treatment might make it go away. This wasn't received as the good news I thought it was and she reacted silently. It wasn't spoken about after that for a while. Eventually she told me that what she loved about me was my personality so if my personality was wrong, what did that mean? Did she know who I was? At the time, I was disappointed by this reaction, but over the years, I have come to see what a fundamental question this is. If you can't work out where the symptoms end and the person begins, how can you know if you're loving a person, or enabling a symptom. What does it say about you, if you're in love with a collection of symptoms? What does it say about your brain that you want to be subjected to that collection of symptoms? If there's literally a book somewhere that says these are the objective criteria for diagnosing a broken brain, where do you put that? How complicit are you in stopping them from being healthy?

However, at that point, all I knew was that the diagnosis made her uncomfortable and I knew her feeling uncomfortable could lead to me losing her, so I never talked about it. Talking about BPD is, unfortunately, one of the ways you deal with it. So Mick stayed inside, undiscussed, while I did no work on dealing with it. Addiction was a thing we could talk about but wasn't the real problem. Now I had the real problem, we couldn't talk about it.

I parked the diagnosis in a bit of my brain and left it alone. I didn't look into it because my psychiatrist told me not to. My lack of ability to do things on my own time for my own interests made it easy not to look into it. And of course Mick didn't want me to know about it, either. He is far better at his job – manipulating me to the point I'd kill myself – if I don't know about the levers and buttons he's pushing.

Besides, I had a panto to get on with where my mum lives and I stayed during the run. My first panto voluntarily, permanently sober. Apart from the couple of years preceding this where I was drinking and/or doing drugs, I would manage to maintain sobriety during panto, both because I had enough to occupy my brain that Mick didn't have the chance to suggest it and because doing panto to hundreds of screaming kids with a hangover is no fun at all. The fact I had done those recent pantos unsober was a benchmark that things were going downhill.

I was a bit more relaxed at panto than I'd been before. My performances improved, I was more relaxed onstage and I tried writing stuff for the panto, which I'd not done before. Previously I had involuntarily been doing a version of my dad on stage during panto but now I was starting to put more of myself into it and starting to untrain those learned tics to become a separate entity from him.

Sara got a massive role. It would mean a month of rehearsals in London in January, then months on tour. I stayed in the hotel with her at that time and things improved. She was happy that she was working and I was just carrying on existing when she wasn't in the room. As I didn't have an area all to myself – even alone in the hotel room, Sara would be back eventually – Mick didn't have a decent arena to work on me, so he was pretty quiet during this time.

At this point, I was financially reliant on Sara due to not having worked. She gave me a card of hers to buy daily items like food. Again, this echoed the parent/child dynamic of our relationship. As a kid, Mum would lend me her credit card until I abused it and she took it away again. I never felt guilty or concerned about this arrangement. Mum had paid my bills as a kid and now Sara was taking over that role. It was an arrangement I had relied on for more of my life than I hadn't. Because of this, I'm sure I didn't really express gratitude for her help. I wasn't ungrateful but I do know I was so used to living this way I didn't express the gratitude she deserved.

Once Sara went on tour, I was in the flat on my own. This gave me some control over my own life again. I could make plans to visit her while on tour, I had to organise my daily life: pay the bills; I had to wash my own face and everything. All funded by Sara, but a level of autonomy. It was an exciting time but this was because Mick recognised he would finally get some alone time with me while she was away.

When I was with others – Sara or family – I would be as grounded in reality as I was ever able. I was clean and sober and looking after myself, I was on Twitter saying normal stuff, so I was doing well in their eyes.

No, I fucking wasn't.

Not that I knew this. I thought I was fine. But when I was on my own, almost as soon as Sara left to go on tour, I started performing a magic show in my head. Whenever I was on my own, I would disappear into this alternate reality. I wouldn't have been able to rationalise it and wasn't actually planning a show. I can now see that I was reaching back for the last thing that had helped me cope before the drink and drugs. I was disappearing into a perpetual performance.

From childhood I'd always put on music with headphones and pretended to do shows. Especially finales. I do love a finale. Running down the stairs at the end of the show to accept the raucous applause with humble, appreciative bows.

I could rehearse that in my head literally for hours. I would cry over and over again with gratitude as I took the bows. Rewind the bit of music that would play as I accepted the ovation and feel the actual emotion time and time again. The ability to access that emotion – not remember it but inhabit it, believe I am in that moment – is frightening. I'm as happy in that imagined encore as I am angry when I recall a road rage incident.

Hey . . . Presto?

While I'd always performed magic shows in my head, I had never done it to this degree. I wasn't aware that I was beginning to live in two separate realities but, over the coming months, the new reality began to grow and grow. But I never mentioned it to anyone and when anyone else was around I didn't have access to it.

In a different context, this wouldn't automatically have been a bad thing. I wasn't working, so developing a show myself would be productive. Write some routines, look at the practicalities of putting it together, give it a structure, rehearse the tricks. Sensible, responsible, self-starting stuff.

But this wasn't about logic. I can now see this was me disappearing into a place I could be alone in. There was never a point where I could have performed the show. It was happening outside of a place my rational brain had access to. The only way it connected to the real world at all was in my absolute certainty that I needed proper equipment.

As a teenager I had stolen my mum's credit card and bought magic tricks from an American website. Of all the bad things I have done, this is the one that still catches me unaware. At the time, I had no foresight about what I'd do with them or what would happen when it was inevitably discovered. Knowing what happened last time wouldn't stop me from doing it again. I knew logically I'd get found out, but there were no branching additional thoughts of consequence, guilt, etc. to suggest I should stop.

At no point in my life have I not known right from wrong but I had always been missing that associated *feeling* that stops the action. So each step of using Mum's card to buy these tricks had a single thought without emotional connection. Open website. One thought. Get Mum's card. One thought. Order a £600 trick. One thought. Each isolated from any emotion.

Once Mum found out, all of those thoughts and emotions arrived, all at once. Guilt and shame and embarrassment and regret and all the rest, all bundling through the door to say hello. I'd feel devastated, especially because they'd arrived all at once so I had to juggle them all at once. It looks like a performance, feeling bad because you got caught rather than feeling bad you did the thing, but I can only tell you that wasn't the case. All of those things were held back from me until they were forced upon me by my mum looking at her credit card bill – and then they all occurred to me and knocked me over. And my inability to connect these actions to emotions meant that, when I did it again months later,

I had to learn that lesson all over again. And because my mum's way of dealing with family problems was to treat each crisis as new information, that got reinforced. And we just never examined it.

Mum always dealt with the problem immediately in front of her and this often meant she dealt with it without necessarily looking at the wider cause and effect. It's like gardening when they say you have to dig down to get the actual root out. You can just keep getting rid of the surface weeds but eventually . . .

It mattered I was stealing, not what I was stealing for. She would pay off the debt, I would endure the telling-off but nothing would have really changed between then and my next theft. It finally stopped when Mum actually tried to punish me. She told me that any earnings from performing kids' shows would go straight to her to pay back what I owed her. I stopped doing kids' shows immediately afterwards so there were no earnings for her to recoup her losses.

The show brought together lots of the things I'd lived with alongside the drink and drugs. Living in my head, not examining those thoughts, inhabiting emotions, not telling others what I was thinking, no forward planning, wanting to be liked, no impulse control, being solitary, looking for something that would make it worth being me.

My former ability to start and stop living a life on stage in my head disappeared and eventually every minute that wasn't with other people or doing basic living tasks was spent in this entirely dissociative state. It filled up the space available, and having told nobody else there was nothing to stop it. But it occupied no thoughts when I was doing something else. I didn't think about it while I was with Sara. As far as I was aware, when I was in the flat I was busy not doing drink or drugs, being normal.

Some physical evidence existed. Scribbled notes or notes on my phone. But the thoughts about the show didn't link from one day to the next, so they didn't add up to a story. If I woke in the morning and saw 'Elephant – hula-hoop?' on my phone, I'd just think it was a bit weird and move on without examining why it was there. Like waking up as Jekyll not knowing what Hyde had been up to last night.

This was accompanied by looking at magic tricks on websites. Here's something you should know about professional magic tricks – they are unbelievably expensive. You know how expensive you just imagined? More expensive than that. A single six-sided die can set you back $1,600 and that's not even at the higher end of the price scale. And the more normal an object looks, the more expensive it is because it's hiding more things it can do. When a magician pulls a rabbit out of a hat they really hope you applaud because the hat probably cost more than your car.

Though it wasn't happening in the rational part of my mind, I was overcome with a feeling that I had to have equipment. And whenever I buy anything I start with the most expensive. Even in this entirely irrational state, I was still certain that I had to have the most expensive tricks, because then they would be the best tricks because just me wouldn't be enough.

What happened next is the thing that came as close to killing me as anything, even stepping over the rail of a bridge or swallowing a whole bottle of pills. It was another crossroads that my brain presented me and asked if I was sure I wanted to proceed and I said yes. I said yes. I have to completely own the fact that I said yes. But, to be honest about that, I have to be honest about my previous statement that I wasn't taking any ILLEGAL drugs.

There's a school of thought that anger isn't a primary emotion. It's a defence, an attempt to not feel an emotion you are threatened by, that you don't want to feel – sadness, or fear. The anger that I would often feel was obliterating – it literally allowed me to disappear within it. I am sure that's not a coincidence. When you are an adult man, screaming in a rabbit onesie, you have to face the fact that somewhere, at some point, you never learnt to deal with certain emotions and feelings. I have come to think of Mick in this way. He's a toddler, screaming, bashing his hands against things, desperately trying to get what he wants. We never learnt how to do that in a functional way and so many of the things I have done stem from that. We don't let toddlers make big decisions for a reason. You definitely shouldn't give one the keys to your life. Mashing handfuls of drink and drugs into your mouth, smashing up your life.

I have been in therapy for a long time. I don't want to be that person who evangelises about it. I have not always been honest and committed to the process. I have not always found it useful. But now, when I think about the process of uncovering things, bringing them out of a place where you aren't aware to somewhere you can be, it feels like a kind of magic. But real magic; not built on lies. You don't make someone look one way, you actually make something appear into your life that was invisible. You give yourself the chance of changing how you behave.

Chapter Eight

Chronic Feelings of Emptiness

Out of all of the symptoms, this is the only one that seems to get described in exactly the same way wherever I look it up. Chronic. Feelings. Of emptiness.

It's like poetry, isn't it? The other ones seem medical, like you could apply some test to them and work out if you had it. But this one? Feelings of emptiness. Firstly you're feeling an absence. Which is tricky to begin with. And not just the normal fleeting feelings of emptiness that presumably everyone feels. Chronic feelings are the problem. You're feeling them for too long, too often. You see that phrase and you wonder what is the threshold – it's essentially telling us that some amount of feeling empty is part of the human condition. I tend to think of it as the one that sits there under everything else. My inability to be with myself came back to the unbearably loud echoes in my empty self.

I was 11 when I first realised that something was a little wrong with me. Because when I thought about Nanny Ett dying, I didn't feel anything. I loved her. I didn't want her to die. I knew I loved her and I would miss her and I knew her death had upset other people but, as I sat amongst my family, watching them crying and looking distraught, I knew

I wasn't feeling what they were feeling. I knew I wasn't feeling anything. More than that, I knew that me not feeling anything in that moment was *wrong*.

Death is the only thing that's certain in our lives that isn't tax or wanking. It's a weird fact for us humans to grapple with really. I mean, not for the dead person, but it can be unspeakably shit for the people they leave behind.

Even though losing somebody is as much a part of life as living it, we don't talk about it.

It's just too awkward (and I feel awkward in Greggs asking if the sausage rolls are hot, so this is a fucking nightmare from my end). But we only really talk about death when somebody's died, and that's an issue because then there's no opportunity to have a more general chat other than at the cremation with three cousins we haven't seen in years and a random butcher at the buffet afterwards.

Speaking of funerals (and the laugh-a-minute riot that they are), I would like to tell you about the last one I attended.

We lost Grandad Joe (not Nanny Ett's husband – the other side) on Good Friday in 2019. As a Christian of Italian descent, he believed in heaven; it was just typical of him to get there on the only day Jesus was definitely out.

I've never understood why we say we've lost somebody. To me it implies we had something to do with them not being here anymore, which is obviously bollocks. Grandad Joe's not missing. He's not hiding behind the couch.

I've lost a few people – not only Nanny Ett and Grandad Joe, but Grandad Jim and friends and other family too – but I can find always find them again. They have plaques and gravestones and memories that let me know where they are.

A memory becomes a memory because, good or bad, it made me feel something when it happened.

I don't get to pick the stuff that I feel, but if I *do* feel something, that thing immediately becomes a memory.

Then, my brain has a choice.

Up there, I have two boxes. One says 'Forget it forever', the other says, 'Forget it for now'. The memory goes into one of them.

I am not informed of the outcome of that decision. I don't pick which box it goes in. I'm never told, and I'll only know if I've forgotten it if my mind reminds me to remember it.

When we say we've lost somebody, it is because we've lost the opportunity to make new memories of them.

The definition of loss is the feeling of grief for a person or thing that is badly missed. To lose something, you have to be able to miss it. One day I'll be lost too, but I'll be found in the memories of the people that knew me while I was here.

You probably didn't know my grandad. You don't know how he talked, and you don't know what he looked like (he was essentially a longer, fatter version of me in case you were wondering), but even though you didn't know him, right now, you're thinking about Grandad Joe, and that is the most alive he'll ever be again.

And that's enough, because right now, you know who he was.

Sometimes, though, my memory box goes awry. I wake up for one day, or three days, or three weeks or three hours, and I just feel nothing. It makes memories difficult. It makes days slow and painful and challenging, because I'm not feeling the usual emotions in response to what's happening, and it makes me more of a struggle to be around.

So I started learning how to pretend to have emotions in situations where those emotions were appropriate. I also learned to feel a deep sense of guilt that I had to pretend at all. Chronic emptiness with BPD isn't the absence of a particular emotion in a particular circumstance. It's just not feeling anything at all. Even when your Nanny Ett dies.

There is an exception to my memory box rule, and an exception to where I stop feeling entirely: love.

I love my grandad. Not loved, but *love*. I continue to do so, even though he's dead. In order to remember something, you have to forget it first.

And I will never forget that I love Grandad Joe.

I am 29 years old and, one day a week, my job is to travel around 30 pharmacies to buy boxes of over-the-counter sleeping pills. I have to do this because pharmacies will only sell you one box at a time and I am taking four boxes a day until my limbs feel like someone else's. At exactly the same time I am doing this, I am feeling very good that I am no longer drinking and taking illegal drugs. (I told you we'd come back to that word illegal.)

It had started slowly at first, in that gap when I'd first left Focus, before filming had started. They didn't affect me massively so I upped the dose to the point one night I took six. This robbed me of my ability to move my legs. I was very aware of how heavy they felt, like I was hypnotised. I stared at them for an hour, then I'd forget why I was staring at them, then remember again, on a loop.

And then one day, I looked out of my window down into the alleyway where people went to buy drugs, presumably heroin, and my head for the first time ever said, 'Heroin? Why not? Give it a go.' So my brain decided that a sensible compromise would be to abuse over-the-counter sleeping pills.

I had tried other drugs over the years – ecstasy, weed, ketamine and so on – with varying results. They either didn't work well with me or I enjoyed them, but the common factor was that they didn't offer the oblivion that I was really after and that alcohol and cocaine provided.

Pharmacies are strict with them – only one packet can be bought at a time. If you ask for a packet you have to have a chat with the pharmacist before they'll let you have them.

So I had a little chat and I bought a box. While I didn't consciously plan to abuse them, in a week I went to double the dose, every single night whether I was tired or not.

Within a couple of months, I was taking twelve a night, which is a massive escalation. I'd take six, wait for the weird buzz to kick in and the odd sensation in my hands to arrive, then take the other six for the weird feeling of my body curling into myself like when I did coke. Taking them in two stages was me being sensible – don't take all twelve at once, mate, you'll put yourself in harm's way. Just sensibly take six times the dose then do that again an hour later, like a grown-up.

Taking them in this amount very quickly requires you to buy them from multiple pharmacies and the knowledge of this makes you aware that this has clearly become a problem. A packet of twenty should last you weeks even if you take one at night, which they tell you not to. If you turn up three days later, faking a yawn and asking for another pack, they will notice and they will refuse.

It didn't take too long for Sara to notice the effects the pills had. Slurred speech, hunched shoulders, forgetting thoughts between having them and being able to articulate them.

One evening she had been staring at me for a while, which I hadn't noticed in my locked-in state, and having watched my twitches and prolonged silence eventually asked what the fuck I was doing.

So I said I'd had a sleeping pill. One. A partial admission at best but she couldn't get angry at me for taking over-the-counter tablets in a way you're meant to. She advised that I clearly didn't react well to them – which was true, just not in the way she meant – and told me to stop taking them.

So a few days later, when the same behaviour returned, she reasonably asked whether I'd taken 'a' pill and I immediately lied and said I hadn't. Indignantly denied it, as I thought I could get away with it. By now she was away a lot touring, so it made these denials a lot easier, though not entirely believable.

Even though she was away working, she'd still want to FaceTime and text me, and I wanted to crack on with the first lot of sleeping pills as soon as possible, 6 p.m. ideally, so those two plans for the evening were not even slightly compatible. I'd try not to take them when we were together, not always successfully, and she'd always notice those failures and we'd argue. But she was unhappy that I was taking the couple of sleeping pills she thought I was taking because that's what I'd told her, not 40.

Like with the cocaine and alcohol, there was no game plan, no perceived way this was going to work out. Just the usual pattern of ad-hoc deflection and deception that kept the immediate addiction going. And so long as I could keep this very wobbly path going, there was no reason to stop. Any night I was alone I would take the pills because they provided the same oblivion alcohol and cocaine did.

The massive doses of over-the-counter sleeping pills, combined with the massive amounts of antipsychotics, antidepressants and mood stabilisers I'd been prescribed, did not make for the healthiest of brain chemistries.

This was the context me planning a magic show came into. Looking back now, I had completely lost track of what reality was, my brain at this point being such a swamp of competing chemicals and bad wiring that it was fertile breeding ground for the worst thoughts imaginable.

I reached a point where I would take up to 40 pills a night. Not always, it would depend on circumstances how quickly and how hard they would hit me. Some nights were merely a 12-tablet night, like having a salad with dinner instead of chips to feel like you're being heathy. On a 40-pill night, I'd have ten to start off, the earlier in the day the better and depending on how much I'd eaten, and see how that first course went.

When that started to wear off, because my tolerance had reached a point where a dose that would put a hippo in a coma didn't last for more than an hour or so, I would take ten more and see where that took me. Forty would be the most I'd need to give me the level and length of oblivion I was after. Forty of the tablets they advise to take once a day and not every day.

The weirdest thing was that they kept me up all night. Most mood-altering drugs I've taken have the opposite effect they have on everyone else. I could do cocaine for two days and not say a word to anyone, the polar opposite of your chatty lager lads doing a few cheeky lines in an All Bar One. And 40 sleeping pills ensured I didn't get a wink of sleep. I should really have asked for a refund.

I got a presenting gig on a children's TV show and entered an identical pattern of behaviour as my days taking cocaine while working. Control it as much as possible so I could do a 12-hour day of filming then, as soon as I was alone, batter my brain into oblivion until it was time to go to work again. And when I wasn't working, the non-oblivion hours were lived in a state completely removed from reality, planning and purchasing for my imaginary magic show.

Even with us living largely apart, there was no way to keep this from Sara indefinitely. I can sit like a twitching goblin, necking handfuls of tablets in a Holiday Inn as much as I like, because there's a Do Not Disturb sign you can hang on the door handle. Not so at home.

The pills removed me from myself, shut me down as an active person. I needed two boxes a day, and the fear of running out produced the same dread as running out of coke. Monday became the day I did my run for the week.

Six hours straight, driving for over a hundred and fifty miles. Bought with cash as much as possible to hide the purchases. A friend's wife works for one of the big pharmacies, ordering stock for the stores, and I do wonder whether I ever appeared on their Excel spreadsheets as an inexplicable sales blip in the southeast for the brand I favoured.

One trip would cost hundreds of pounds. Cheaper than coke, far pricier than alcohol. A mid-tier-cost addiction made pricier by the fact I had some twisted snobbery towards not buying own-brand generic tablets with exactly the same drug in them. I wouldn't be seen dead taking something that wasn't my brand, even if I might eventually be seen dead having taken them, if my addiction continued to spiral.

I'm such a fierce addict that I managed to take an over-the-counter drug used by stressed shift workers and people who to have a kip on a plane and turn it into as destructive a force in my life as cocaine ever was. The lies, the planning, the paranoia, the escalation and the cost – physical, emotional, financial – this little blue sleepy pill beat me into oblivion just as hard as anything *Scarface* could offer. I tell you all this not to excuse what I did next; I take full responsibility for that.

I am 29 years old and I have done a really fucking terrible thing. Even in the context of thinking that a lot, this time it's different.

My mind revolves around this event.

I can't remember a day I haven't thought about it, and my past and present are split between everything I did before it, and everything I've done since, and it's the only thing Mick knows I can't defend.

There are no jokes here. I'm just going to tell you the thing, because the thing isn't funny.

I want you to imagine someone you admire and care about. Someone you have known for a while. Someone you respect. Now I want you to imagine that, at their most vulnerable, you betrayed their trust. Even knowing what they were going through. Knowing exactly how bad the place they are in is because you too were there recently. Even knowing how it was only the kindness and care of others that kept you alive. You did it anyway.

I did this.

I stole money. And this time it wasn't £600 on mum's credit card. This was enough money to put a deposit on a house.

Anything that ever happens, good or bad, Mick reminds me about this in order to ruin a good day, and make the bad ones worse. Every text that's not responded to, every time somebody doesn't pick up the phone, every time I see somebody I haven't seen for a while, Mick reminds me of this event. Five years on, it's the reason I can't accept compliments, and the reason I can't get to sleep at night.

Another rehab phrase I couldn't stand at the time is that 'secrets keep you sick', but I can confirm that it is not bollocks. It's true.

I am sick. I'm sick and tired of being sick and tired of Mick hurling this at me, because he knows it's indefensible, but I have to do something because I'm pretty sure I'm the only one that's still thinking about it every day.

I've spent years successfully keeping this a secret, but here I am, telling you when you haven't even asked.

I did that. And I live with that. I know that nothing I can do or say can ever make that better. I realise that I am not the important thing about this situation. Though I know there is no way they would ever be reading this book, a big part of me wants to apologise here, to say sorry.

I told you that I was writing this book for me, and that's true, but I'm telling you this because I know you, too, have got a worst thing you've ever done. It doesn't matter if your worst thing is worse than my worst thing or better: if you can't stop thinking about it, everything else is irrelevant.

I can only move on from the things I create if I let them go. I don't feel like I deserve to let this go, but thinking about it is essentially self-harm at this point, and maybe, if I start talking about my worst thing, you might feel OK enough to start talking about yours. I have to start believing that I am not the sum of my worst days, but I spend every good day thinking about the worst one, and that has to change.

I don't know how this is going to go now, how you'll react, but it's important for you to know that.

Two important things, here:

I AM NOT ASKING FOR SYMPATHY.

I AM NOT BLAMING MY MENTAL ILLNESS.

But we've spent some time together by now, and it's not an accident that I'm telling you near the end of this book. You obviously don't hate me because you're still here, which means you've listened and you care. Thank you. Your opinion might change here but it's a risk I've got take for me.

Would I have done the thing if I didn't have Mick? Fuck no. But I've always known right from wrong, and I knew this was wrong, I just couldn't feel it at the time, because knowing something is awful but doing it anyway is a symptom.

I know that none of this context makes any of that better. I don't expect forgiveness.

This is where the model for asking for forgiveness in rehab's twelve steps ultimately loses me. My need for forgiveness is not louder and more urgent than their need to be left the fuck alone by someone who did something terrible to them; my narrative that I was a different person when I did those things, a sick person, a person in thrall to addiction, someone working through symptoms of a mental health condition, is no excuse.

That narrative only works if you're in my head; if you know that's genuinely how it feels. The person who did those things had my face, and my voice and they knew the things I knew. Back then they told lies that sounded a lot like the things I say now, frequently. And I betrayed that trust then. More than that, I used that trust to steal. My actions at that time look a lot like those of a calculating psychopath. But I had no forward planning abilities to do such a thing, nor did I have the learned experience of linking actions with consequences. If it's hard to believe that I wasn't crafty or cold-hearted enough to think this way, it might be easier to believe that I was incapable of carrying out such joined-up behaviour even if I wanted to, which I didn't.

I have to take ownership of what I did in the days and weeks afterwards. Because, as much as I might want to now look back and see Mick's hands in everything, making things the worst they could possibly be, so he could have the best possible run at having me kill myself, I also have to accept responsibility so that I can stop doing it.

I know this sounds bizarre. Unbelievable, perhaps. I get that. It sounds fucking weird to me and it's my brain. And I know it sounds like a justification for what I did. Again, it isn't. I did it. My fault. No argument there. No call for leniency. I did do it, I knew it was wrong, and remembered doing it afterwards. But the 'So if you knew all that, why did you . . . ?' questions you've just started asking were impossible for me at that time. You're applying the rules of a normal brain to mine.

But I now say: 'But this time . . . but this time I'm not lying. This time I'm not protecting the addiction; I'm the real me.'

I get how convenient that feels. How much energy it takes to come back. And to everyone in my life who has done so, I am immensely grateful. But to anyone who can't, I will never ever feel anything but understanding for that. It's not your job to make me feel better about myself.

In the days after I did the thing, there was an ever more insistent voice in my head that the only response to what I had done was to kill myself. This felt different to previous suicidal thoughts I'd had.

The sleeping tablets didn't dampen it down. The voice in my head was sure that the police were coming and that the only solution was for me to kill myself. And, for the first time in my life, I didn't do something to drown the voice out; I started to pay attention.

BPD is a disorder. It's a set of things that we objectively agree aren't working properly. And experiencing chronic feelings of emptiness is one of those criteria. But, as I pointed out earlier, if chronic feelings are the problem then logically some feelings of emptiness are normal. I don't know about you but I find that strangely reassuring. Because it means that the problem isn't the feelings of emptiness; it's when they stop you doing other things, that's the problem.

Chapter Nine

Paranoia and Dissociation

Transient, stress-related
paranoid ideation or severe dissociative symptoms

Ever since I was a kid, I've always known they are coming to get me.

The details have changed over the years but the certainty hasn't. When I was a kid 'they' were monsters under the bed and the reason they were coming is because I was a kid and getting kids is what monsters do. It's their job. Now, I overtake someone on a motorway and I catch their eye in the mirror and I think they recognise me and they think I'm a twat. I am certain in that moment that they have a deep abiding fascination with me and all the things I've ever done. And that they think I'm a right twat. My earliest memory of paranoia is when I was nine. I had a *Batman Forever* poster on my wall, and I was convinced that Tommy Lee Jones was watching me. For years, every night, I thought that the actual Tommy Lee Jones was either real and inside the poster, or, at the very least, had a camera fitted into his eyes so he could watch me from his home. I never told anybody because I knew it wasn't real, I just felt like it was.

Imagine that childhood certainty that if any part of you shows above the duvet, they're going to get you. Well, I feel that now. They're still coming to get me, it's just the *them* that's changed. Drugs paranoia was particularly bad. If I was on my own, I would construct an elaborate series of *Home Alone*-style traps at various places around the flat, so that if someone was coming to get me, I would get early warning. One night I spent eight hours hunting down the murderous elves I'd convinced myself had invaded the flat.

Unless you've had coke hallucinations and paranoia, you can't grasp how completely real they are to you in the midst of them. There *were* elves – murderous elves – somewhere in the house and I had to find them before they got me. I couldn't see them but I could hear them. And their knives. Armed with my own kitchen knife I went on an elf-hunt and checked every room in the house. I had to approach each room really slowly, otherwise they'd hear me. Obviously. God knows what I planned to do if I actually found them. But I would creep up to each room, slower than a continent drifting, to try and catch them out. Whenever I opened the door of a new room I'd flick the lights on, trying to catch them unawares like little pointy-eared cockroaches, but they were always too quick for me.

Drugs at least had the benefit of identifying who 'they' were. In my head the police were always poised with the battering ram and the handcuffs, waiting to cart my sweat-drenched, heart-pounding, elf-panicked body off to jail. It's good to put a face to your paranoia, even if that face is a copper shouting your right to remain silent at you.

But what's drugs paranoia without the drugs? I often think there's someone breaking into my flat now. I know rationally that is very unlikely, so now I lie awake at night listening to what my house not being broken into sounds like, so when somebody *does* break in, I'll know what it sounds like better, which I know is fucking insane.

The drugs have gone but the paranoia remains the same and the fear it brings has never dimmed. I've spent thousands of nights awake, listening for the front door to open and the tell-tale creak on the stair signalling that this is the night they finally come to get me. I still wedge suitcases against my front door every night to slow them down. And I know precisely that stair that always creaks as the flat settles for the night. Yet I know that nobody has ever burst into my room to get me. Nobody has any reason to.

And I know every night none of that matters, because here at last is the terrifying moment when it will happen like my brain has always told me it would.

I'd get a dog for protection and for company, but I'd be paranoid the dog was in cahoots with them, too. (If you think about it, someone must have set up a guard dog company where they train the guard dogs to respond to a secret command that you can buy from that guard dog company for loads of money.)

There's a link between thinking that people are watching you and imagining a specific 'they'. Paranoia and dissociation are linked, because to feel the full force of BPD paranoia it requires a certain dissociation from reality. You can't have too great a grasp on the real world if you think Granddad Jim is watching you all day.

Granddad Jim died when I was a kid and I thought it would cheer Mum up if I said I'd seen his ghost. Flowers might have been another option but I went for ghosts instead. She asked what the ghost was wearing and, by sheer dumb luck, the outfit I invented for the ghost I hadn't seen was exactly what they'd buried him in. This convinced the family that Ghost Jim existed and I was asked to retell the story so much I started to question whether I had actually seen him.

My brain took hold of this information and decided it meant that Granddad Jim was watching me. All the time. It shows how severe my paranoia is that I don't believe in an afterlife but I do believe that Granddad Jim is judging what I do. I honestly thought Granddad Jim could see what I was doing, and that I'd better not think a bad thing because that might make me do the bad thing and if I did, Granddad Jim would see me do it.

I am 29 years old and for the first time, I am thinking about the voice in my head who tells me to do terrible things as a separate person. This voice is what I will eventually name Mick as a way of personifying my BPD.

I have started doing this because Sara has told me that I will have to live with what I've done for ever and I am trying to explain to her how my brain has been working. I realise that I can't live with what I've done. Every day, there had been a voice in my head, reminding me of what I'd done. Reminding me of how awful it was and how the only real solution was to kill myself.

Part of me was beginning to think the reason this had happened was because this was the most destructive thing possible. If someone had wanted to make me act in a way that most fucked everything up for myself, this would be what they'd do. Despite the tablets and the steak knives and the bridge, this was the very first time in my life I felt suicidal. Truly, presently, constantly suicidal. This was the first time I was aware of a voice in my head very clearly and precisely saying, 'Kill yourself.' A continuous, tireless voice that elbowed its way to the front of the queue of all other thoughts telling me to end things.

It was different from thinking I was going to kill myself. The previous incidents were me feeling like I'd had enough of whatever bit of life I was going through at that moment and I was tired. Once the moment had passed, it stopped being part of my thoughts. It's like when you get to the end of a big meal and your brain says, 'Stop eating'; it's a reaction to a series of events rather than an active part of you. But my brain was using that voice to say I should stop living.

This period of time was the best chance Mick has ever had to kill me. When he suggests suicide because I've missed a train or run out of melon, it's easier for me to go through the process of dismissing that as an option so he'll show me what my other options are. But when he suggests it because I did the worst thing I've ever done, that becomes a lot harder. And he makes that argument to this day, on the few occasions I feel good about myself or receive praise. Somebody thanks me for something? 'Yeah but you did that, didn't you?' Happy with a piece of work I did? 'Yeah, but you did that terrible thing.'

And I'm not asking for sympathy on the basis my punishment is that I have to think about it a lot. It's not enough. I'm simply explaining that it never goes away and never should. Like an addict remembering how bad things can get, I have to constantly remember how bad I can get if my brain is allowed to do its own thing.

Then there is a phone call and I realise that I am not going to go to prison. With a generosity I am unable to fathom, they have said if I repay the money they won't press charges. And Sara has paid the money, which is the entirety of her savings.

Now the paranoia has shifted to people I know finding out what I've done. If someone is ten minutes late, it's because they're finding out what I've done. If I don't get a reply to a text message immediately, it's because they have been told and decided to break all contact with me. And there is the guilt that Sara had to pay this because I couldn't. Because every penny of money I had ever earned had gone on drugs and booze and rehab (and more recently boxes and boxes of over-the-counter sleeping pills).

The guilt that I have hurt so many people is overwhelming, and all I have to show for what I've done is a variety of very expensive pieces of magical equipment. I never wanted them, I don't want them, so I list them at very low prices so someone else can buy them and I don't have to be reminded about what I did. This will eventually cause a high-ranking member of the UK magic community to tell me off for tanking the expensive magic trick economy. But all of this has to come to a head at some point. For a couple of months, I lurch on, a mess of guilt and sleeping pills and a voice telling me to kill myself. There are constant rows with Sara who cannot understand how there are even more lies in our relationship, who cannot understand why I am only just now understanding what my behaviour has been like, what it has done. The trust has gone and I spend every moment sorry for what I have put her through and resenting how I cannot think about anything other than the money I owe her and what it represents. The voice in my head fixates on it, uses it as evidence that there is only one thing I can do.

I am 29 years and 364 days old. I have driven to get myself a celebratory McDonald's. I get to the turning to my hotel but take the wrong turn and end up on the motorway. I loop back up and down the motorway to get to the hotel turning and do the same thing again. For over two hours, I cannot make myself make the turn for the hotel; every time my hands keep turning the wheel back onto the motorway.

I pulled into the hard shoulder, the hotel visible through the bushes, wondering why I couldn't make my car turn left when I needed to. It wasn't the car, it was me. I gave up. I stayed awake sat on the hard shoulder, called the hotel at 6 a.m., the earliest decent time I could call. They walked from the hotel a few hundred yards away, climbed through the bush and drove my perfectly functioning car back to the hotel. It was the first time my brain had physically manifested itself this way. The person who drove me back did so while looking at me like I was crazy. I can't blame them; I was.

I went back to Sara and told her that I needed to sort myself out and I needed to be alone to do that.

Please know I am very aware how unfair and ungrateful that sounds. She had spent a lot of emotional energy, time and all her savings stopping me from self-destructing. Stuck around way past the point most people would have had every right to leave.

I am under no illusions that I was no picnic to live with. I wasn't even half a bag of stale Haribo sitting on the floor of a multistorey car park. But I couldn't do what I needed to do as part of that relationship, with that history. And I wasn't making her happy, because how could you be happy with someone so demonstrably broken. She needed me to be someone else and I needed to be someone else but they were different people.

You can't stay with someone because of guilt; it's not an emotion to build a relationship on.

We split up on the day of my thirtieth birthday and though there was that fuzzy period at the end of a relationship where one person tries to restart the relationship then, once they stop, the other one starts trying to rekindle it, we eventually stayed apart. I take out a series of loans and pay Sara back.

I moved back home with Mum, fat, unhappy and full of sleeping tablets. She had taken on the role of guarantor to pay Sara back what I owed her. I am aware of how this looks. One woman taking on the financial and emotional load of the man-child. The debt literally being transferred across without me even having to touch it. And it's a fair cop. And here's that knot at the centre of recovery. The egotism of forgiveness. I have to believe that the sequence of events that will lead to me finally becoming and staying sober were worth it. But no one else does. The process of self-actualisation is just selfishness from one angle.

To the person making the omelette it was all worth it, but if you're the chicken who laid the eggs, almost certainly not.

Back home, things do not magically become better. I'd not told my psychiatrist about my new addiction. I'd pretend

I was going to bed at 7 p.m., which didn't fool Mum for a second, and while taking the pills I'd go and make myself four rounds of toast. Eat them. Then forget I'd done that, so I'd do it again. When it got to the stage of me eating most of a loaf of bread while she was asleep, my mum called my psychiatrist with her concerns.

The only two ways out I could see were to kill myself or relapse and I knew that if I went back to cocaine or alcohol, I'd kill myself. Two slightly different roads with one destination.

The amount of sleeping pills I was taking by this point was starting to feel a bit overdose-y. I'd lose use of my limbs and fall flat on the floor, the sinking feeling increasing even after I'd landed. My body's tolerance had reached its upper limit and I vividly remember a couple of moments where I thought, 'Oh shit, too far, this is it, I'm going to die', when another couple of tablets might have made that fear a reality.

I started ordering sleeping tablets online from less-than-reputable websites. The reliability of the tablets that would arrive was a gamble to say the least. This was in addition to my shopping trips to real pharmacies. Adding this random factor into my already heavy tablet use accelerated me to reaching the point of no return. Also, because my one justi-fication – it's over-the-counter tablets so it's fine – was no longer valid. This is the same trajectory as all addiction in the end.

Re-rehab

Mum was crying one night. When she feels scared and helpless, she has an expression I've not seen often but can't mistake when I do. She reverts to a child: tearful; feeling completely unable to do anything. She'd been seeing these parcels arrive and was fully aware what was in them. She confronted me about having taken these dodgy tablets, ignoring my denials with good reason. She told me I had to stop, because she was scared to be around me when I did take them. Scared for me and scared of me.

I told her to phone my psychiatrist and lay it all out to him so he could form a plan. I didn't know what that plan would be but I submitted myself to whatever it was. I used my 30 seconds of honesty to let Mum know the true extent of my addiction before the *Countdown* music finished and the shutters came up again.

There was a Fancy Rehab centre nearby (there's a few around the country – they're like Greggs for rich addicts) and, much as I hated the idea of going there based on past experience, it was where my psychiatrist was based, so this is where it had to happen. They suggested weaning off the sleeping pills as the recommended route but I decided to go immediately to zero. Any medical side effect could be treated by the staff on-site and I knew the addict in me had to have his toys taken off him completely. The prescribed medication would have to be tapered off, so that's what we agreed.

I knew what Fancy Rehab can and can't do and what they can and can't tell you. They may make you think you have to follow the treatment they offer but if you've paid them your several thousand pounds a week, the relationship is customer/company not doctor/patient. This allowed me to set my own terms of what this visit to rehab required.

On day one, they pushed the treatment brochure across the

desk at me and I pushed it back and told them I needed to get off as many drugs as possible in the next month because I had to start filming a kids' show. In my head, I explained this with a steely determination, but, in truth, I was a bloated, bearded, slurring mess that was probably barely coherent.

But I knew what I needed was to learn how to be in a room, on my own, with nothing else to do. And here was a safe environment to learn that without access to a pharmacy or a dodgy website. This was my plan and, because the card payment had cleared, that became their plan.

I'd never felt safe around me, with good reason, so I actively practised being safe, with myself, in a room on my own. A core belief in rehab is that time on your own is dangerous so this was the one thing they'd never let me do, despite it being the very thing I needed to learn how to do. Huge parts of my life, with the work I do and the personality I have, are spent alone.

Telling me in rehab I can't be on my own was pointless because they were telling me that in order to get better I had to stop being me. And while I hate myself and wouldn't mind having a go at being someone else, I also know that's not possible. So rather than tell me it's not something they advise, I needed them to accept it's going to happen and teach me some skills to do it.

To an outside observer, my intensive therapy involved sitting in a room, on my own, with a TV on in the background. Not noticeably different from a bloke in a doctor's waiting room but exactly what I needed to do. Alongside this was the immediate withdrawal from the sleeping pills and the start of tapering off everything else, in a room, safely.

It was shit and I hated it, even though I knew I was doing something productive, even if it didn't look it. I had to trick my brain into learning how to not take sleeping pills and I knew I couldn't do that in an environment where that was an option. Hard as it may be to believe, there were few physical effects of going cold turkey on the sleeping pills. I thought my body would notice that the daily punishment beatings had stopped but it didn't seem to.

I never drank enough to trigger physical dependence on alcohol, and cocaine is psychologically addictive rather than physically, although there is often an odd reaction three weeks in where you get very sick, like your immune system has emerged from its shell and is simultaneously catching up with all those jobs it's been putting off for years.

What I was trying to do was to create a habit, a habit of sitting in a room with myself and not doing something to obliterate myself. I knew I was a creature of habit. If I have a can of Coke, I have to run my index finger round the can once, open it, then do it again. A lot of the habits I'd created were terrible but now I had to trick myself into a new one that wasn't. A fortnight dry run of living in the real world within a medically monitored jail.

Wherever I go, *I'm* there when I get there, and that was the thing I'd never addressed. How to sit there with me in a way that wouldn't eventually kill me. I had to stop being shocked that, whatever habit I kicked, I was still me afterwards. I didn't do drugs or alcohol at work, nor when I was around other people, because they gave me a reason for existing that I had never felt I had when I was on my own. A room with a TV and my phone and nothing else in Fancy Rehab was a close simulation of the hotel rooms and living rooms I'd be in by myself for however long the rest of my life was.

I had no idea if this was going to work and it was a gamble that could fail badly. I knew I could form habits when it was a physical thing in the world rather than a thought process or an emotional response, so sitting in a room could be another physical habit to form. That was the logic. I'd tried so many different things and had always behaved like an arsehole and wanted to kill myself, so dealing with me with no substances involved was the only solution left.

I felt like doing the usual rehab for the sleeping pills would have got rid of that and left a gap for whatever thing came next. Dealing with that rather than dealing with me would have just kicked the problem a year down the road. The cocaine, alcohol and sleeping pills weren't the disease, I was. So I had to treat that rather than whatever symptom I swallowed or snorted next.

You're trained to look at the similarities between addicts rather than the differences and that makes sense because 'No, but I'm different' is the standard reason not to stick with rehab and therefore relapse. It's hard work and there is no substitute other than learn to live with the life you have now, prepare for it to get worse or die. Nobody goes straight to the shop doorway with their first drink or line but that's where you will end up if you don't do the work. So I get that saying 'But I'm different' to the 'Don't be alone in a room' mantra can look like shirking that hard work. But it's just being realistic about the settings your rehab is going to take place in.

Another reason the previous rehabs may not have worked for me is that, unlike those people sleeping in doorways due to addiction I mentioned earlier, my family never left me. Ever. Because they cared. So I never lost anything, for so long, other than personal dignity and certain relationships, I didn't lose anything. Not jobs, not family, not personal freedom. And help was always there whenever I needed it or was ready to accept it. Classic rehab says I never hit rock bottom but rock bottom is person-specific and unfortunately I was treating rock bottom as a challenge. After every rehab I knew I could fall further. Even the worst thing I ever did I couldn't blame on addiction and couldn't call rock bottom through addiction.

Rock bottom, by the way, is potentially the worst place to change your life around. You can't truly change until you get to rock bottom, you're told. But after crashing through all those floors, I was knackered. I just wanted to lie there and be left alone. I was covered in dust and bruises and scratches and the remains of a toilet I'd hurtled through somewhere on the 13th floor and this is when they wanted me to be at my strongest? That wasn't where I was going to make my best long-term planning.

But I did reach the point where I knew I had to change me rather than just treat the addiction or this would keep happening. I left this final stay in rehab clean of sleeping pills, tapering off the prescriptions by one medication at a time (antipsychotics then antidepressants then mood stabilisers), and with a two-week rehearsal of being alone. It would be another month before all medications stopped completely.

*

I am 30 years old and for the first time in my adult life I can watch my thoughts with nothing to alter or dull them. I was dissociated but with an awareness of my dissociation I'd never had before. It is essentially the first time since I was 16 that there was nothing floating around in my system. Without anything exterior added into the mix of my head, I realised that I didn't always agree with my own thoughts. I remember that occurring to me very quickly and I remember not panicking. I just realised that this was, well, a bit weird. Mum had always told me that I was a good person with a good heart who just fucked a lot of shit up. I easily agreed with the final bit. I wasn't a good person and I could prove that with all the awful things I'd done to myself and others and nobody who'd done those things could possibly have a good heart. But this new distinction – between my own thoughts I agreed with and my own thoughts that I didn't – showed a possible way of making all three bits simultaneously true.

But for that to happen, I had to find a way to do this next bit.

Because it was like a computer game where traditional rehab had told me that drugs and alcohol were the final bosses and if you learned the correct fight combo moves to beat them, you got to put your initials into the high scoreboard and walk away. Instead, when I finally did that, the arcade machine started glowing, grew seven times larger and a whole new set of buttons and joysticks appeared. I hope you have enough pound coins, Mick said; now the real game starts. There was this voice. There was a kind of hope to it but it also made me feel unfixable.

The problem was that I was the problem. I was fixating on external things – over-dependence on work to compensate, drugs, alcohol, relationships – when essentially, the problem was me. Or rather, the problem was within me.

I'm not a patient person. I want an immediate fix for a problem. I was in my early thirties before I used an oven for the first time because needing food and waiting 90 minutes for food was frankly unacceptable when I live opposite a McDonald's where there are people who will give me food now. It was like finally making the decision to cook yourself a meal, switching on the oven only to realise that you're going to have to rewire your entire house first.

I made the decision, a gamble really, that I would not attend meetings. It was a gamble that learning to be on my own in a room was what I needed in order to stop another addiction turning up. I stopped taking the sleeping pills and eventually I stopped taking antipsychotics, adding another layer of newness to the situation.

I'd been putting 150 mg of stuff into my body that was making me into somebody else. Somebody less likely to kill himself, perhaps, but not the actual me. If I wanted to work out who the actual me was, so I could work out how to stop the actual me from killing myself, I couldn't do it while on medicine that hid him away. Again, I am very aware of the danger of seeming to advocate stopping medicine a mental health professional has prescribed. However, I'd never had a lot of faith in the prescription drugs to do things to my brain, or at least not good things. I'd been taking them for years and still wanted to kill myself all the time, after all, so I didn't feel much attachment to them.

No longer being on the tablets gave me the ability to dissociate and unplug from my life and thoughts and examine them from a less emotional position, allowing me to ask not just what I was thinking but 'OK, *why* are you thinking that?'

The medication I stopped taking is designed in part to stop things like dissociative thoughts as well as the other negative aspects of BPD but the downside for me was I didn't get to choose which of the symptoms it targeted. Each medication seemed to target a different bit but not others and there was no way of knowing until the dosage had been whacked up.

This in itself would be a partial victory I might have accepted but the tablets also dulled my ability to fight the things they didn't deal with. Imagine going into a boxing ring and you've managed to nobble the fight by tying one of your opponent's arms behind his back but as a result you've tied yourself to a chair. My best chance was by being completely unmedicated, feeling the full onslaught of the BPD but also having as mobile a brain as possible to fight back.

Finding Myself
What happened was that, for the first time in years, I was alone with my thoughts.

Imagine a bar in a cowboy film, filled with the worst dregs of the Wild West. This was where the chaotic thoughts in my head had always taken place, bandits and renegades throwing chairs around my psyche, smashing the place up while throwing booze down their throats and laughing at the damage it caused.

I walked into this saloon bar inside my own head, which made all of the scarred, shifty patrons stop to see who this newcomer was. I could look around as the piano went silent and look them in the eye.

There are so many different bad thoughts, negative emotions and terrible ideas that Mick wants me to experience and each of them now populated this *Deadwood* bar like a Friday night after a gold rush. And every one of them is Mick. A full bar of Micks, all with a different malevolent thought, some wearing a hat or a fake moustache or an eye patch so they can pretend to be somebody else. One table muttering about doing cocaine again, a sleepy-looking guy with a box of pills, the piano player concocting a plan to steal something and a guy at the end of the bar waving a bottle of Sambuca at me as I sip on my soda water.

I understand this can be difficult to imagine and I certainly know it can sound like an excuse – it's not me thinking and doing these bad things; it's this bar full of criminals all called Mick – but everybody in that bar is Mick and ultimately Mick is me. That voice telling me to do something terrible that is going to make me want to kill myself, that voice became Mick.

Having a clear head had its downsides and one of them at this point was realising how depressed I was, the depression having previously battled to get itself noticed amongst everything else. I still am depressed and suspect I always will be. When people say they have BPD and depression, it's like saying you have TB and a cough. Of course you do.

I have a base level of depression even on my best days that means my brain has a bit of air let out of it. The depression is separate from the suicidal thoughts, which come from the

BPD although they can interact with each other. Like a load of wasps on a poisonous snake.

Around this time, I went on Lorraine Kelly's talk show to talk about suicide for the first time. I'd written an article about my mental health that was published in the *Metro*. I'd never heard anyone talk about my type of suicidal thoughts, where it wasn't a result of your lowest point in life, it was just a Thursday.

I'd tweeted it on Suicide Awareness Day. Lorraine Kelly and I followed each other on Twitter and despite it being something I'd never normally do I messaged her to ask if she'd share the article I was planning to tweet. She very kindly agreed and invited me on the show the day I was planning on tweeting it.

I was still quite raw from rehab and still learning how to be a human being and talk as myself so here I was, having a go at doing it on a live breakfast TV show. I promised myself I wouldn't pre-prepare any answers and reminded myself when I got anxious that I had asked for this by putting myself forward. And it was another way of living life in full honesty.

Another thing I was acutely aware of was that there was no follow-up plan to this interview. Basically, I wasn't selling anything. Every time I'd seen a celebrity talk about mental health on TV, the interview would always wrap up with the viewers being reminded of when their book/tour/album/commemorative tea towel was coming out. This was the point I always mentally checked out when I saw those interviews because subconsciously I dismissed everything that went before as a sales pitch. I know breakfast TV isn't the place you go to for serious psychiatric help but I took it personally that nobody ever talked about this stuff just because it was stuff that needed talking about. I am aware of the irony that if things go very well, I will probably end up sat on a sofa, talking about mental health and then they'll hold up a copy of the book you're holding. All I can say is that I won't get in a taxi, go to another studio and talk about something else. Ever. This book is about mental health because that's what my life has been and is always going to be about. Because for any of it to mean anything, there has to be something other than briefly depressing the market value of magic equipment to come out of this. I don't think I'm some holy fool, here to bring back wisdom. But I do think that, whatever the exact sequence of events are that have brought me here able to talk about what goes on in my head, I owe it to the people that have suffered because of what I've done, to try and do that honestly.

I had a weird moment in the taxi home after *Lorraine* where all this came into focus. That maybe I wasn't an entire arsehole and maybe I might be able to do something that would hold off killing myself. The trick was to try and keep this going and continue not being an arsehole as much as possible. You can be alive and not be an arsehole.

It was like being in a forest and a deer walks into a clearing. You don't want to do anything that will make it run off. I was very aware that I shouldn't open my mouth and say something stupid that would make it all crumble. This is why expressing happiness is so hard, because even expressing that it exists might be enough to make it go away again. And talking positively about myself is the hardest thing I can do.

I assume nobody cares about my life and Mick assures me that they don't. The BPD doesn't want me to talk about positive things about myself and it has taught me to divert any conversation I'm in away from myself just in case I have to be positive.

I opened up about suicide and BPD because I wanted to match up who I was in every environment including work. I knew if people had found out everything I'd done, my life would be over. If I started talking about my brain, it would at least be a safety net if people knew a bit about me first.

I feel that continuing to talk is my only option, because I've tried feeling like I'm the only person in the world who is this like this and it hasn't worked. This option might not work either but it feels like my best chance. The more I understand how my head works, the more open I am about the worst things I've done and the more light I shine on Mick, the more cornered he gets. It's worked so far in the smaller ways I've gone about it, balls-in, so it's time to go balls-out.

I'd started doing my Twitter videos at that point about mental health but I'd not really incorporated humour into those videos. With most of my videos I have a rough idea of what I want to say but it's not heavily scripted. For this one I tried to act out in my head what happens when people try and minimise the seriousness of what's going on in someone's head and I did it in the form of an argument with myself.

I remember watching it back and, as well as being pleased that I could use humour in these videos, it suddenly struck me that the thoughts I have in my head are like they're being said by somebody else who sounds and looks exactly like me. I could only make that connection after seeing it on screen.

It was the first time I felt, if not at the steering wheel, that I even knew I was in a car with Mick at all. I'd been locked in the boot while he went for a joyride but slowly I could start taking a bit more control of things. Not the steering wheel, certainly, not at this stage. But at some point maybe the gear stick or even the pedals. For now, I could turn the little overhead light on or off and that was a start.

This was what was missing when I did the worst thing. I knew what I was doing was wrong, I've always known if what I'm doing was wrong. But because I hadn't put the work in to try and be something better and because I was smothering my brain with tablets that made this work impossible anyway, I didn't have the referee in my head to look at a thought and make a decision about what to do with it.

The ability to do this – recognise what is a 'me thought' and what is a 'Mick thought' and recognise that the Mick thoughts are usually Very Bad Ideas, so turn them down – is what started the process of me feeling that, while I had spent a large part of my life being a complete arsehole, maybe a future where I was less of an arsehole was possible.

Thoughts aren't things. So long as I don't enact the thought, it's not a thing, it's just a thought inside me. If I keep doing the work that stops the thought becoming a thing – and I know if I slip and allow it through to my hands and mouth I will absolutely do that bad thing – then it's just a thought. I have to carry around those thoughts but that's my burden rather than the world's burden and carrying that burden is what I need to do to stop me from being the worst me.

The Penny Dropping

Here's a thought that was groundbreaking to me at this point in my life that may seem obvious to you: in order to not kill myself, I could stop doing awful things that make me want to kill myself. There was a world I could exist in where I stopped doing these dreadful things that made me want to kill myself. And that started with recognising that I was always, always going to have thoughts that I didn't agree with.

I think it's why other people with BPD, who through no fault of their own can't do this, can feel that there's no point in carrying on living. Because they must be an awful person to think and do such awful things and they don't want to be an awful person any more. The devastating thing about suicide is that you feel like you're the good bit killing the bad bit inside you. It's the complete opposite, but by then it's too late to realise. I just wish I could emotionally recognise this as much as I could logically recognise it.

Somebody, at least one person but probably more, is now reading this sentence thinking, 'There is nothing you can possibly say that avoids the fact, Joe, that you're a criminal for what you did and I don't want to hear your excuses to justify yourself.'

While I don't disagree and I can't justify it or expect forgiveness, I have to make something positive come from it because if I don't, I'll die. I can't stop that it happened but I can try to stop it from happening again. It has to be the engine that keeps me from being that person again, the AA meeting in my head every day. And I have to do it in a way that doesn't tip over into self-pity or self-hatred.

Undermining any effort to be a better person is the self-hatred. If I didn't have the self-hatred, I think I could cope with the rest of the symptoms but because it's always there, it's always digging tunnels underneath any foundations I make to try and improve. Self-improvement is no easy feat when you think you're trying to improve a complete arsehole.

Again, this is why me talking about my thoughts often robs them of their power.

I'm in a relationship with my own thoughts and it's not always a great one but it's the longest relationship I've ever had. It's one I have to learn to live with because any external relationship I have will suffer until I do. The old cliché says you can't love others until you learn to love yourself. Bollocks. I have so much love to offer people because I'm not wasting any of it on myself. I'm needy as fuck but I have a lot of love for you to spare.

People with BPD are sometimes called psychopaths but it couldn't be more different. If a psychopath had lived my life so far they would be feeling absolutely fine with everything I've done because they lack empathy. Having BPD doesn't rob you of empathy; it just holds it back from you when you need it the most and gives you it back once it's too late. Mick is a psychopath, or would be if I let him.

That year when I was doing panto, people would speak to me in the street to thank me, rather than just say hello or they liked what I did. It was partially due to the videos I'd been doing on Twitter and partially because in this panto I tried to do something a bit different.

I struggle to understand why people thank me. I'm just doing stuff and people are enjoying it, I appreciate that and I'm really grateful for it but I struggle to make the leap of thinking it's something I should be thanked for. It doesn't help that my life feels like I'm in a film due to the dissociation. Nothing that's happening is really happening. *The Truman Show* with more cocaine. I know logically it is happening but there's enough distance there for it not to feel completely real. So to be thanked for things that aren't really happening or I haven't really done feels odd. Which is not to say I'm not incredibly grateful whenever it happens.

The slight absence of reality makes it easier for me to talk with complete honesty about me and my brain because the stakes are lower if it's not really, completely happening. The opposite of an internet troll, rather than hiding myself to spread dishonesty because I fear the real-world repercussions, I try to be completely me in order to be as honest as possible because there isn't an entirely real world for repercussions to happen in.

When I see somebody famous clearly going through a rough patch talking a couple of weeks later about how they're on the mend and feeling much better and happy to help people going through the same stuff, I wince. Because that's the time you're at your most vulnerable and in no condition to think about looking after anyone else but yourself. It's such an unpinned hand grenade to play with so I get why everyone just pops the pin back in and walks away from it.

I know the words I say have a power and weight to them and my dissociation sometimes stops me from realising just how loaded they can sound to others and how harsh and blunt they can appear. People don't say they want to kill themselves in everyday life. When I joke about it in real-life conversation, I can see people at a loss over how to react. That's why doing it as films and sketches helps, as it creates a distance that stops the burden of reaction from either of us.

And this is my approach to my brain and how I talk about it publicly. Again, my approach and nobody else's. Talking about it in a personal capacity is the polar opposite. Don't wait until you think you won't kill yourself before you tell anyone. Tell somebody you trust as *soon* as you realise you're thinking it.

On my worst days, I hate that I've done this because I really, really want to kill myself and now I've done something that stops me from doing it.

It was only when I took those toys away that, after a bit of a sulk, Mick found all the other bad ideas to suggest instead. I was parent to the worst child in the world in my head and I'd previously dealt with his petulance in the worst way possible by giving in to his addiction tantrums. Once I started trying to be a proper parent to him and took those away, it was a lot harder. Ask anyone with kids if getting their kids to eat vegetables is easier than giving them the junk food they're screaming for.

Mick is essentially the child in me that never got out. I was never a child as a child. Always around adults, never around kids, treated as an adult without any of the benefits or tools of maturity. None of the opportunities for those childhood bad ideas to be played out, suggested, tried, failed and learned from in a way that wouldn't kill me.

We get those developmental years as a chance to learn all that and I missed them, so now the Mick in my head is an adolescent who's never learned restraint or compromise or self-preservation or patience or empathy. 'I should've been allowed out when you were a kid. Now you're stuck with me.' He's up there, grounded in his room, for ever, and he's never going to be happy with that.

Chapter Ten

Me

I am 31 years old and my girlfriend Holly is filming me in her parents' garden as I wear her big sister's childhood leotard and shout names for dance moves. It was the first very weird thing that happened in a year that ended up being filled with very weird things.

I am one of a very small list of people who can class 2020 as the year that their life changed for the better. And I mean small – it's just me, Jeff Bezos and the nice Welsh weatherman who played the theme tune to the news on his brother's drum kit. It was arguably the most globally traumatic year in generations. But so far it was going very well for me. Which isn't to say all of the massive issues relating to my BPD had gone away but, at the start, Mick was certainly taking a break while I tried to work out what the fuck was going on

This chapter isn't named after one of the symptoms because it's about how they all happen, all at once, tangled up, complicating and amplifying each other. If you want, you can play a fun game shouting out the different symptoms when you spot them. (Though probably not if you're reading it on the bus.)

Mainly this year was going well because I had fallen in love.

Which was complicated. Not only was I an addict with a very obvious mental illness at the start of a global pandemic, in Yorkshire to meet the parents of a woman I'd met doing panto a couple of months back, but – and this will shock you, after reading 65,000 words of my thoughts and fuck-ups – I'm not actually very good at understanding relationships.

I know they're a thing, of course. I know because I have some. I'm a son, a boyfriend, a brother, an uncle, a cousin and a friend. A relationship is something independent, that lives between the two people that made it. You might not believe that your relationships are worth a damn – but they are fixable, if you work out where they've gone wrong.

To illustrate this, I'm going to use a hopefully not-shit metaphor to demonstrate how much easier it is to understand something you can't see if you imagine that it's something you can. I'm going to replace the word RELATIONSHIP, with the word BUCKET.

Imagine, if you will, a dark, empty room. In the middle of the room is a big, bright, white bucket.

The BUCKET is the RELATIONSHIP.

If you and I decided to have a BUCKET, we agree to put it between us, and share the contents.

I fill half of it with some of me, and you fill the other half with some of you.

OUR BUCKET has two rules. It always has to be full, and it always has to be 50 per cent me, and 50 per cent you.

If somebody needs something from the BUCKET, they take it out. But every time you take something out, you have to put something back in so that it stays full, and stays equal.

Problems grow when somebody keeps taking things out of the BUCKET but stops putting things in.

Then one person is putting everything they can into the BUCKET, but they're not getting anything out of it because there's nothing left to take. It's empty.

Relationships start to corrode and collapse when they stop being cared for by both people. If it's not equal, it won't work.

Relationships are real.

I know I can't see them all the time, but I know they're there. And I know they are fixable.

Mick and the Parents

I struggle in other people's houses and other people's spaces. I don't feel I belong anywhere at the best of times and this is heightened when I'm in somebody else's home. I feel like I stick out. I'm constantly on edge. When I'm not concentrating, I have a habit of folding in on myself, going full Gollum. I didn't know how to be in front of Holly's parents because I'd not been in a relationship before where I'd tried to be authentically me all the time.

When I want to impress somebody in a personal capacity or have them like me, I clam up. I sweat and my knees shake, which has the opposite effect of what I'm after. As time has gone on, around Holly's family, these behaviours have got worse rather than better because Mick knows I want these people to like me, and he knows what I think will stop that from happening: a mute, shaking, sweaty man in their living room.

If I know we're travelling up to see them, he'll make sure I have something to obsess about for seven hours beforehand to rob me of my energy and my ability to be normal around them. I spend the entirety of the M1 worrying how her mum Sue will feel watching me put eight packs of cocktail sausages into her fridge. She wouldn't mind. She'd probably find it funny. But I feel like she'd think it was worse than me kicking one of the cats. The fact I still want to visit them because I care about them and Holly means he's trying even harder to make me feel worse when I do. It's the standard pattern with Mick. He's found a toy to hit me with and the more I take it away, the harder he'll try until he realises that he's not going to stop me, at which point he'll find something new.

When I first started down the long road to understanding myself, I tried every trick in the book to help me. But it turns out that, apart from therapy and rehab, a lot of it just doesn't stick.

You'll note that I'm putting this in the last chapter of my book for a reason, but the books were the worst. Oh god, the fucking self-help books.

Sara used to buy me books, and it was incredibly well meaning of her. She was trying to help, but it didn't. It made me worse, because when I did try to read them, as far as I was concerned, they were full of shit, and they made me feel more unfixable than I did before I picked the bloody thing up. I read *The Secret* three times, really hoping something would click, but it never did.

Of course it didn't. I've got a personality disorder. Trying to fix my brain by writing a gratitude list is like trying to remove a tumour with a fucking spoon.

It's fantastic that the general worldwide conversation about mental health has broadened, and people are talking about anxiety and depression more freely, but what that's done is sanitised the mood around the subject. It's created a world in which feeling sad is something that can be fixed by going for a jog, and your anxiety can be relieved by spending 30 seconds looking at a picture of some nuts. If it works for you, brilliant, but guess what? I can't stop thinking about killing myself; to say nut photos don't touch the sides is putting it lightly.

Do you get people sending you memes? I used to wake up in the morning to texts from my mum, with a picture of a beach and 'You don't find a happy life, YOU MAKE IT :-)' written underneath. Thanks Mum, but the only thing that's done is remind me that I'm more mental than the rest of the world, because everybody loves that shit, but I look at it and feel guilty that the help you're trying to give me isn't enough.

So I either have to say, 'Please don't send me this shite' and upset you, or say, 'Thanks, love it, smiley face emoji' and let them think they're making a difference when really they're making you feel even less understood. I wouldn't recommend the second option by the way, that would be a lie, and as we've seen, if you lie to somebody about the help they're giving you being enough, it keeps you on your own. If you're thinking about killing yourself, we know that's not a good place to be. You're better off saying thank you for trying, but they really don't help me. Or if you're the person sending them not getting much back, maybe ask them if they like receiving them. Sometimes, just knowing somebody wants to help is help enough.

I think the other thing I struggled with when it comes to self-help books is the fact that they all seemed to be coming at the issue from an angle of 'This is how shit my life used to be, but now it's great, and YOU CAN DO IT TOO', without any real world advice on how to not kill myself. It's great that you sorted your life out and wrote a book about it, mate, good for you, but I'm not thinking about how good my future could be, because I don't think I'm going to have one; I've not even decided whether I'm going to do tonight yet, let alone March, and there is no amount of strangers being reflective about their own problems they've sorted that is going to make me feel like being alive any more is worth it.

I never found a book that said that.

There is now a book that says that.

That might be for a reason though. It might be because I'm the only person in the world that's ever thought that. I wouldn't know, because, as ever, you're the first person I've ever told about that feeling. But I also know there's a chance that you just went, THANK FUCK IT'S NOT JUST ME.

I'm still really fucked up. I know a lot of this book has been me looking at my past and the shit that I've done, but I'm not sorted. The problem is still here, I just handle it differently now, and I do less stuff wrong, because I treat the problem.

The problem is me.

The day I worked that out and stopped feeling sorry for myself was the day I actually had a chance of surviving what goes on in my head.

I'm actually quite boring and sensible, it's Mick that's the screwed up one. But as much as I talk about Mick being a separate entity to me, he's not. He's my thoughts. Not all of them, but he does a fucking good impression of me.

Twinkle Toes

On that first visit to Holly's parents', I managed to be more or less OK. I'd not met her family before, and we were due to go up for a couple of days. And our stay went well. The day I was meant to leave I was delaying my departure for as long as possible because I wanted to squeeze out every last second that I could with her.

Holly's a dancer, and we were watching a dance tuition video on Instagram. The instructor took viewers through some moves in his front room with all the furniture pushed back, narrating as he went.

At one point, he mentioned that the move he'd just done was 'Hand Towel'. I couldn't stop laughing. The *what*? The hand *what*? This was the funniest thing I'd seen in ages.

I had a dance move I used in panto I called 'The Reverse Otter', which, as you can guess, is an impression of an otter going backwards. I knew I could add others – 'The Beef Toe' – into a complete routine. The idea of sincerely doing a dance routine, and sincerely telling an audience the silly names of each position is not anything close to my idea. For as long as people have danced, they've called their movements by ridiculous names, from Roy and HG to Steve Martin. Even Bob Fosse had shit names for moves – 'soft boiled eggs hands' was an actual thing.

I asked if Holly had any dance outfits in the house. She found a couple of her sister's old leotards in the loft. I squeezed myself into one, and I assume from this point forwards it became *my* leotard, because there was no way Holly's sister would ever want to wear it again, no matter how many times it went through the wash after I'd shoe-horned my gooch into it.

And this is how I heard that the country was locking down – standing in Holly's parents' back garden with my feet stuffed into child-sized split-sole jazz shoes.

I ended up staying for four months. What happened in that time will stay with me for ever. I spent more time with Holly's family than I've ever spent with my own as an adult. They learned an awful lot about me during that time, not because I was telling them but because after I tweeted the dancing video, things got a bit bizarre.

Within a few hours, it had got 400,000 hits from all across the world. Countries who had no idea who I was, places I'd never been or performed in, people that *definitely* didn't know I was joking. It was a mad experience watching the view count roll upwards like that clock in Times Square that counts the national debt.

The next morning, the view count went into the millions. I woke up to a message from the *Metro* from a friend of mine, Duncan Lindsay. Coincidentally he was the first person I contacted when I wanted to talk publicly about my mental illness. I'd read an article of his a few years before, and it was the first time I'd read something about someone's broken brain that felt like it was written for someone like me. He'd reached out, asking if he could get a quote from me about the video.

I was dealing with several things at once. A video having gone viral, a request for comment from a newspaper, and the small matter of the world tipping upside down. I'm not great when things are ticking along as normal, and things were very much Not Normal. A disease that people didn't know much about and didn't know would ever be conquered was catnip to Mick, who sat back to see if this new guy from Wuhan could finish the job he kept trying to start.

Bob, Holly's dad, had asked her how the video had gone so she showed him the *Metro* article, which was mostly about his daughter rather than me. There must have been something in it that prompted him to say we should make more videos, although I'm sure he regretted that when I kept using his office to tell Lorraine about them on national TV. Or *The Morning Show* in Australia at 3 a.m. Or *Good Morning America*. I spilled my guts out to strangers around the world and Holly's parents must have heard it through the walls of his office.

The cost of keeping me in their home for that amount of time must've been equivalent to keeping a thoroughbred at Chelmsford Equestrian Centre with full livery, so I'll always be grateful to them for that. They are some of the nicest people I've ever met and, given that my family had always been a bit separate from each other, it was wonderful to see them love each other as much as they do. Holly will always be one of the best things that's ever happened to me. I left their house a better person than I was when I arrived, and living with them truly showed me what it means to be a family and I gladly spend every day hoping to make Holly as happy as she makes me.

Showing 'Me'

Being with Holly has taught me how to navigate being a person with BPD in a relationship in a way that doesn't terrify the other person or make your BPD worse by being dishonest about it. Just because you're fucked up, doesn't mean good things can't happen to you.

However, telling somebody you have a voice in your head that wants to kill you, that you think about suicide all the time, and that you have to consciously process thoughts, emotions and actions because you have no unconscious regulation of those processes, is not like letting them know you're due to inherit the family billions or that you have a Shetland pony living in the bottom of the garden.

It's not Tinder profile material and if somebody decided it was more than they could deal with, I wouldn't blame them. But, as much as I would have loved to pretend it wasn't there, I knew it wasn't going away and I knew that I couldn't avoid having this conversation with Holly for both of our sakes. I really, *really* didn't want to do it but knew I had to. I had to protect me from starting a relationship with somebody who wasn't prepared to deal with a brain like mine, and I had to protect Holly from starting a relationship, then finding out what was lurking inside my brain.

To deal with that as graciously and acceptingly as she did is beyond my understanding. I'm not sure I could have done it.

Credit to Bob and Sue too. They never once brought it up. They let me know that they'd watched the TV spots I'd done, and from that I took it to mean they knew about the problems with my brain because that was usually the topic of conversation in those interviews. The feeling was that they knew about it and, if I wanted to talk to them about it, they would be fine with that.

Despite that, we've never sat down and talked to each other directly about Mick and my wonky brain. They must have questions, I'm sure, but I don't want to force them into a conversation they're not ready to have. It's like a Mexican standoff of politeness, neither of us wanting to make the first move for fear of upsetting or offending the other.

There's a large part of me that's grateful they've never asked though. The things you can't see are difficult to explain to somebody that doesn't have any experience of that thing; made even more difficult if you know the words, but don't know which order to put them in. Even if you can explain how you're feeling, you might be scared to tell anybody else in case they don't believe you.

Arguments occur more frequently when they're about something you can't see, because if somebody can't see something, it can be denied. Unfortunately, mental health problems fall into this category too.

If it's invisible and you don't understand it, you have a choice. Accept that it's definitely there because other people that know what they're on about are talking about it, so trust them, listen to them and learn from them, or be a dick.

'Nope. Not real. Can't see it. Prove it.'

I'm not saying I don't understand that thought process, because I really do. How do you believe something you can't see and know nothing about? I get it.

Nobody's having a row about air though. I can't see air. I don't know anything about air, but I know it's real. I'm sure people have tried to explain it to me in the past but I didn't pay attention because I don't care. But have I died of suffocation yet? To Mick's eternal sadness, no.

I know that air's everywhere without understanding it because enough people are talking about it. For my whole life, I've heard people talking about air. I've heard enough people that are air experts talk about air that I accept air is a thing, even though I can't see it, and I'm comfortable trusting somebody that knows what they're on about to accept that it's a fact.

But you know what I'm not doing? Kicking off at Professor Brian Cox on Twitter, telling him that I don't believe his whiny opinions because I can't see it, so he must be an attention-seeker whose career is essentially a tapestry of desperate and unsubstantiated air lies. Pics or it didn't happen.

That would, obviously, fall into the being a dick category. He knows. I don't.

I can't see it. But I know it's there.

I try not to think about this, unsuccessfully, but Holly's family must have an opinion about her being in a relationship with somebody like me. Maybe it worries them. I think if I had a daughter, I'd probably want her to be in a relationship with somebody who doesn't think about killing themselves every day.

They are great with me. Genuine, warm and open. If lockdown had happened at any other time, without Holly and her family in my life, I don't know where I'd be now, or even if I'd be here now. That's the difference it made.

What it also showed me is that I need more in life than just work and not killing myself. My biggest problem has always been that time between work finishing and work starting again. That's where and when all the bad things happen. The things I did on Twitter – whether it was doing a daft dance video or talking about suicide and BPD – could be that thing. They were work in the sense they might lead to actual work down the road – and when I make the videos, I bring the pride in my work and my skills to make them look as good as I can. But they were more than work. They were things that could take the place of me pretending to be someone else, or doing magic tricks. I could be honest in every room I was in.

Everyone had their lives turned upside down during lockdown and, overnight, performers lost their entire reason for being. It often felt during lockdown that entertainment and the arts weren't necessary – that was certainly the message pushed by those in power. But, if anything, those months showed the exact opposite. It's what makes the rest of life worth it.

When you die, they may mention what you did for a living, but it's what you loved doing that they'll talk about at length in order to define who you were. And that's so often films or books or poems or songs. You never want to be at a funeral where someone's great skill at accountancy is the abiding memory of them. The very last memory the mourners will have as they leave your coffin behind is a song written and performed by somebody the people in power thought didn't matter.

You can be told the arts aren't viable but after you're dead the only thing you leave behind to show you were there are the things you loved and the things people loved about you. I think about death, my death, all the time. And now I think about what will be left behind when that death happens. I can say that whatever happens, I've written this book. I've tried to make someone out there feel less alone about their suicidal thoughts, or more able to understand what's happening in someone else's brain. I have decided that I want to spend my time making things that make me feel less alone. You should too.

It's why doing this book matters. To put this out there. To say that feeling that nothing, including you, matters isn't something only you have ever felt. That allowing the bad thoughts in your head that aren't you doesn't need to define you. That having a brain that hates you and shows this via addiction or depression or suicidal thoughts or BPD isn't something to stay silent about.

Between the Sheets

I've been trying to write this book for years, ever since I spoke about suicide on *Lorraine* and she suggested I write a book about it, because Lorraine is wise, so if she tells you to do something, you do it.

What didn't help was that my original title was *I Hate Self-help Books*. Any time I got into an email conversation or a meeting room with somebody in publishing, they would eventually ask what my idea was and if I had a name for it. These were usually publishers who dealt almost exclusively in self-help books and I was asking them to publish something that said the rest of their publishing was bollocks. And at no point did I consider changing the title as a way of getting these meetings to go further.

Having no idea what I was doing didn't help either. I had a meeting with a literary agent and my planning involved bringing a load of books with me that I wanted my book to be like. This might sound like a smart move, to discuss the themes, structure and approaches of successful books in the same genre.

But, as I pulled the books out of my bag, I told them, 'I like the front cover of this one, so something like that. And I like the thickness of this next one, so we can make it really thin like this? Under fifty pages, that's really important. And can it be more sort of square rather than the usual rectangle like this one?'

There was never a second meeting.

I'd always been aware of the Chimp Paradox. I say that, even though I have three books about it I've never read, but I knew about it generally as a concept. But, basically, you have shit ideas, you make the shit ideas come out of the monkey, then you can put the monkey somewhere else. Sorry to reduce a professor's life's work to that, but that's what I took from it. Just saved you fifteen quid.

When I was trying to get a book going, part of my brilliant *I Hate Self-help Books* pitch included a gag about the Chimp Paradox, which said that you buy *The Chimp Paradox* and don't read it for five years and then you use the fact to kill yourself. I sent that to the person who actually commissioned *The Chimp Paradox*. Their reply wasn't a happy one.

My chimp became Mick.

Having something to aim for isn't a bad thing in life, because it gives putting up with all the bad bits a purpose. Knowing that you might always be aiming for it without ever getting there, and that the bad things will always be there is OK, or at least less terrible, when you have that. I wish this part of me, the part that hates me and wants to kill me, wasn't the biggest part of me. But it is. I can fight it, but I'll lose that fight, so instead I can make something useful of it instead.

They say it takes three generations for you to be completely forgotten. For the last person who knew you to die and with them the memory you were here. The only way to counteract that is to leave something behind that lasts and to make sure that it isn't the worst moment of your life or the worst thing you did. I've lived my life up to now defining myself by the worst things I've ever done because, rightly or wrongly, I have to. Because you can't do the things to people I've done and not do that, and, if defining myself by those things stops it happening again, that's what I'll keep doing. I can't gamble the alternative. But I don't want to kill myself because I don't want to die alone, and I don't want that for anyone else, and if putting all this down in a book might stop it for somebody then that's something.

You're not alone when the voices in your head tell you you're terrible.

I may end up, after I die, being defined by the worst moment in my life. I can't control that, especially if that's what I deserve, but if I can avoid it by not being an arsehole from now on, that would be nice. Something to aim for. I don't want that to happen to me or anyone else. I want to be defined by something that will last and the only thing that really lasts is love. So now I have something to aim for.

Love.

Thank you for reading my book. Actually, it's not my book any more, it's literally yours. I still hope you're OK.

And please, whatever you do, don't fucking kill yourself.

Ten Things I Love about You

1. You
2. Are
3. Here
4. And
5. That
6. Means
7. That
8. Things
9. Can
10. Change

Appendix

Here is a picture of me holding a chicken.

Acknowledgements

Extracting this book from behind my eyes has not been a one-man event, and I would like to say thank you to the people that have genuinely kept me alive long enough to finish it.

Thank you to Marleigh Price for being my first-ever editor. She gave me confidence that I wouldn't fuck it up when I felt like fucking this up was the only potential outcome. She also taught me that the Korean word for penguin translates as 'business goose', which will always be the best thing that I know.

Thank you to Jamie Coleman, for being my second-ever editor. To say I'm grateful for his patience is an understatement. The only thing you need to know about how brilliant Jamie is, is that he wrote a book called *What I Lick Before Your Face*, a collection of haikus by dogs. Actual thing.

Best £8.99 I've ever spent.

Thank you to Nick Pettigrew for helping me find the right words on the countless days I spent looking for the wrong ones. He is a truly kind human that was never, ever late to meet a person that was never, ever on time.

Thank you to my literary agent Max Edwards, who got in touch one day to see if I wanted to write something and has spent two years helping me do something I've spent years failing to start, let alone starting to finish.

The four people I just told you about are the epitome of how to know somebody like me. Society is, on the most part, supportive of people having a mental illness, until you start exhibiting symptoms of one. Then, if you're lucky, 30 per cent stay, but the rest bugger off without saying bye and they don't even bother asking if there's anything they can do.

The four people I just told you about asked.

Not just once. They asked me what I needed every single day for two fucking years, and they will never, ever truly know how much what they've done has meant to me, and how much it's saved me.

I couldn't have done this book without them if I tried.

And I tried.

Thanks, too, to Simon Hattenstone for interviewing me in *The Guardian*. I always knew I'd be on the front page of a newspaper, I just assumed it would be for something prison related.

Thanks to Maya Hattenstone for telling her dad Simon to interview me in *The Guardian*.

Thanks to Lorraine Kelly for being Lorraine Kelly. I absolutely fucking love ya, Lorraine.

Thanks to Dawn French for being the literal first person to read this book in less than two days even though we'd never met and she had lots of shit to do because she's Dawn Fucking French.

Thanks to Duncan Lindsay for standing up first to say he wasn't OK, then helping me get up there with him. I truly mean it when I say that this book would not exist if it wasn't for Duncan. We've barely met once, he's helped change my life twice, and I will always feel lucky that we were here and broken at the same time.

Thanks to Dr Ron at my mum's GP surgery. He's a fucking legend. I've got his personal phone number. You know you're ill when your GP lets you have his WhatsApp.

Thanks to everybody at Trapeze and Orion, especially Katie Espiner for knocking on every window I ever saw her walk past and to Tom Noble and Alex Layt. Thanks to Donna Hillyer and Kathryn Wheeler for helping me choose the best words in the best order.

And thanks to Sydney James and everybody at Aevitas for looking after me.

Bryan Kirkwood, we've not spoken for many years, which is shit, and my fault. But if you ever come to read this, I will never ever forget everything you've done for me personally. Thank you, and I miss you.

Thanks to Chip Somers. I wasn't always ready to do what you told me, but I always heard you, and I'll always be lucky our lives crossed.

Thanks to Tom Huber, the only therapist that ever looked me in the eye and told me I was going to fuck something up, and told me what to do to stop it. Shame I didn't listen, but I'm glad we're both here now. Tom is an amazing bloke that does a lot of good in the world. If you need help, you wouldn't go too far wrong to get some from Tom. That rhymes. Nice. You can find him at thecounsellingprovider. com.

Thanks to Phil Belfield, my theatrical agent. He is the sweetest man that popped up when I needed someone kind to look after my work business, at a time when my kindness was sensationally thin on the ground. Thanks also to Mark Ward and Laura Swingler for being lovely and never getting wound up by me telling them to say no to somebody that wanted me to be on a podcast.

Thanks to my agents over the years, Bob Voice, Nicola Hobbs, Alex Segal and Michael Ford. I have not been an easy client at the best of times, and I've been a fucking nightmare at the worst. They all played a part in me getting to now not dead, and I will always be grateful for that.

Thank you to you, if you've ever sent me a message online. Since March 2020, I've received over 100,000 messages from people all over the world. Thank you if you've kept me going by reminding me that it's not just me that feels this fucked up.

I don't know why you came across my book, but please know however long you've spent with me, it means a lot. I get a lot of messages from people saying they saw me in a shop or something but didn't want to say hello because they didn't want to disturb whatever it is that I was doing. Please, please, please, if you ever see me anywhere, come and say hello.

The reason I keep telling people I think about killing myself is so that I can't. I'm not scared of myself because I know wherever I am, somebody nearby might already know that I'm not OK. So wherever I am, whatever I'm doing, if you've read this, please come and tell me so I can say thank you.

Joe xx

Credits

Trapeze would like to thank everyone at Orion who worked on the publication of *Ten Things I Hate About Me*.

Agent
Max Edwards

Editor
Jamie Coleman

Copy-editor
Donna Hillyer

Proofreader
Francine Brody

Editorial Management
Clarissa Sutherland
Tierney Witty
Jane Hughes
Charlie Panayiotou
Tamara Morriss
Claire Boyle

Audio
Paul Stark
Jake Alderson
Georgina Cutler

Contracts
Anne Goddard
Ellie Bowker

Design
Nick Shah
Joanna Ridley
Helen Ewing

Finance
Nick Gibson
Jasdip Nandra
Sue Baker
Tom Costello

Inventory
Jo Jacobs
Dan Stevens

Marketing
Tom Noble

Production
Hannah Cox
Katie Horrocks

Publicity
Alex Layt

Operations
Group Sales Operations
    team

Sales
Jen Wilson
Victoria Laws
Esther Waters
Group Sales teams across
    Digital, Field Sales,
    International and
    Non-Trade

Rights
Susan Howe
Krystyna Kujawinska
Jessica Purdue
Ayesha Kinley
Louise Henderson